YOUTH PLAN

Youth Plan Worship
C: YOUTH   No. 1 of 1
S: ~~Studies for~~ Youth MINISTRY
B: Worship & Sacraments
Age: YTH Type: Book

Youth Plan Worship
C: YOUTH   No. 1 of 1
S: ~~Studies for~~ Youth MINISTRY
B: Worship & Sacraments
Age: YTH Type: Book

Youth Plan Worship

Betty Jane and J. Martin Bailey

The Pilgrim Press

New York

The scripture quotations are from the *Revised Standard Version of the Bible*,
copyright 1946, 1952, and © 1971, 1973 by the Division of Christian Education,
National Council of Churches, and are used by permission. Inclusive-language
changes have been provided by the authors. Other acknowledgments appear in
Notes, beginning on page 209.

Library of Congress Cataloging-in-Publication Data

Bailey, Betty Jane.
    Youth plan worship / Betty Jane and J. Martin Bailey.
        p.   cm.
    Bibliography: p. 199
    Includes index.
    ISBN 0-8298-0745-4 (pbk.) : $10.95
    1. Worship (Religious education)   I. Bailey, J. Martin, 1929–
II. Title.
BV1522.B25   1987
264'.088055—dc19   87-17622
                                                                        CIP

The Pilgrim Press, 132 West 31 Street, New York, NY 10001

Contents

Why This Book?

In the early 1960s we wrote *Worship With Youth* to meet a need we ourselves had felt many times as we worked with youth in churches in Iowa, Missouri, Illinois, and New York. As we helped young people with their worship services, we became convinced that given some understanding of the meaning and methods of Christian worship, they would respond with eagerness. We found, too, that worship became more meaningful to them when they avoided using ready-made services from books and instead arranged their own from a store of resource materials.

Now that more than twenty years have passed, and we have changed from youthful youth leaders into middle-aged ones, we have decided that our book is somewhat out-of-date. But we also found that much that had meaning in the early 1960s has meaning to youth today. So we concluded there is still a need for a book to guide youth in planning worship, but it should speak in the vocabulary of today.

We have designed this new book, *Youth Plan Worship,* to be used by both young people and their adult advisers. The User's Guide at the beginning will help you get the most out of the book. Part One will give an understanding of the why and how of Christian worship, while the resources in Part Two will provide a basic selection of materials for use in building services for young people's worship in church school or fellowship groups as well as other groups for which youth might plan.

Although we have dwelt rather heavily on the mechanics of preparing and conducting worship services, we have based our book on the assumption that the services that result from its use will help the young people who prepare and lead them, as well as those who are led, to enter upon a true experience of vital companionship with God.

Betty Jane and J. Martin Bailey
Montclair, New Jersey

User's Guide

If you went out and bought a stereo or a computer and simply plugged it in, you might be able to figure out how to use it. Then again you might not. Even if you did figure it out, unless you read the manual or user's guide, you would probably miss some of the special things your new machine could do for you. You also might really get into trouble if you didn't read the warnings and pay attention to the dos and don'ts.

This book is like an electrical appliance; it is possible to use it without reading the instructions, but it will be more effective if you take your time to get acquainted with what it can do for you. There aren't a lot of warnings and you can't really get into trouble, but as they say in most instruction books, "A little time invested now will save time in the future."

Part One, Planning for Worship, tells how to construct a worship service in terms of specific settings, occasions, and elements involved. Part Two, Resources for Worship, offers a wide choice of prayers, readings, and other material for use in such services.

If You Are a Pastor or Director of Christian Education

This book is designed for youth and those who work directly with young people in planning worship and educational experiences. Although you, as a pastor or director of Christian education, might want a copy in your own library or the church library, it is a good idea to have it in people's hands before a deadline for planning worship arises. A teacher might be interested in planning a worship course or might need help in planning informal worship in the classroom. The leaders of the youth group might find the book useful as they begin to plan the year's work.

If you are working with young people to plan a service, you might have to tap into the resources in Part Two immediately. Try to have the young people also investigate Part One, which means that you will need to take time yourself to become acquainted with the contents of each chapter.

This book can also be used to create interest in worship on the part of an inexperienced worship committee of a congregation. The six-session course for youth at the end of this guide can be adapted for adults. A worship committee might also review the book themselves before recommending it to a youth group.

The book will be least useful if it is used only to extract little bits and pieces for worship services and most helpful if it is used in its entirety.

If You Are a Teacher of a Senior High Class

This book offers you, as a senior high teacher, help in a number of ways. Part One contains a set of chapters for you to share with your young people on how to plan more meaningful worship experiences. Part Two offers a treasury of resources that they can use, adapt, rewrite, or be inspired by. Try to provide enough copies so that everyone in the group can read the book and use it freely.

You can use this book to help you plan informal worship moments in your class, as will be described next. You can also use it to follow a six-session course on worship, which will introduce worship concepts and acquaint your young people with this book as a resource. The course is outlined at the end of the User's Guide.

Short, informal moments of worship can be an ongoing part of the life of your class, reminding the young people of the context in which they study and learn. Such moments also help bind them into a community of support and concern for one another. Informal worship can also help youth explore the meaning of worship itself by introducing them to the varieties of moods of worship, kinds of prayers, and new ways of using scripture and other worship materials.

Brief worship moments can be held at the beginning, end, or middle of a class session, although they are probably more meaningful at least part way through the time the class is together. That way they can be based on the experience the group is actually having. It is better to include such times less often and have them meaningful than to plan for regular times and have them perfunctory. Significant and special times in the life of the group can be marked by somewhat longer periods of worship, but in either situation the format should reflect the needs of the class members and the content of their work.

Avoid the traditional "devotions," in which someone reads an inspirational piece on any old subject the reader happened to find in a devotional booklet. Try to be clearly focused on something relevant to the group. If you use a short reading, help the group to center down first and then read slowly, thoughtfully, and with pauses for thinking time.

A time of silence or meditation can be the center of informal worship. Prepare the group by helping them settle their bodies comfortably and then guide their thoughts with an idea or two. Listening to recorded sounds or music during a period of meditation is also helpful. It is always wise to close off this kind of experience with a short prayer or simple phrase of affirmation or even just "Amen."

Prayer itself can be the main part of such a brief worship moment. Bidding prayers, in which the leader suggests what to pray for and members of the group respond either silently or aloud, are particularly useful in this context. No one should ever be coerced to pray aloud, but as members of the class get to know one another better, they will tend to be more willing to speak.

In the 1970s an idea was developed called Faith Exploration. In its simplest form it is a combination of sharing oneself with others and then looking into the Bible to give meaning to that sharing. Two examples of ways in which this approach can be used for informal worship follow:

1. Have people share experiences of how it felt to be new in a group. Read Matthew 9:16–17 and talk about how this group can both show newness and affirm its roots. Close with a prayer that affirms the old and celebrates the new.

2. Bring a group of everyday objects to class. Let each person choose one and explain in turn why he or she thinks he or she is like this object. Read 1 Corinthians 12:4–7; 12–13. Close with a prayer for the unity and diversity of the group.

An excellent group of suggestions for using the scriptures in informal worship can be found in *Finding Ourselves Christian* (New York: United Church Press, 1983). Some of the ideas include the following:

1. Read a passage of scripture as a dialogue.

2. Have the scripture read by three different people in order to see the different interpretations they give through their inflections and phrasing.

3. Have people share experiences in their lives that the reading of the particular passage of scripture has brought to mind.

4. Talk about what the scripture passage says to the particular group and how it relates to their experiences.

Another source of materials for informal worship moments is, of course, Part Two of this book. The table of contents will help locate materials on some subjects. Checking the calender of resources and index at the end of Part Two will lead you to materials particularly related to seasons and days of the church year. Keep in mind that most of these materials were written for more formal occasions and need to be adapted for informal use.

Some groups find rituals such as holding hands in a circle or singing one verse of a song a helpful way to close a class session. Although rituals are good, they should not be a substitute for exploring a variety of informal worship forms.

If You Are the Leader of a Youth Group

Begin by reading through this book yourself so you, as leader of a youth group, know what is available for your particular group. Let your group know you have read the book and introduce it by using materials from it with them. Make one or more copies available to several young people and then talk with them about ways in which they can include or improve worship within your group.

Chapter 13 outlines the responsibilities of a worship committee for a youth group as well as the role of the leader. If your group is small, one person can be the worship committee and work with you to plan worship occasions in advance. Look over the year as you plan your program and identify times for worship experiences and worship education. List special occasions such as retreats, opportunities for leading worship in the congregation (see Chapter 2), and regular group meetings that could include times of worship. Include some occasion for worship training or exposure to new worship experiences during the year. Make a chart like the following:

Date	Occasion	Type of worship	Person responsible

In deciding on the type of worship and in assisting the persons responsible, check back through the materials for teachers of a senior high class in the User's Guide. You will find some suggestions for informal worship moments that could be used on a fairly regular basis with your group. Sessions 4 through 6 of the six-session course at the end of the User's Guide would also be useful if your group is being asked to plan a worship service to share with the congregation or with a regional youth event.

The worship needs of each youth group vary from church to church and from year to year. Take time with the program-planning group to explore the possibilities of incorporating worship experiences. If there is resistance to including worship, it often means that the group has had too little variety in their experiences of worship or too few opportunities for informal worship. Worship has become either boring or an unfamiliar territory to them. Begin with simple, short, and informal worship moments that you lead yourself, and later incorporate interested individuals into working with you in planning and leading them. As time goes on, introduce these individuals to this book so that they know there is help as they begin to work on their own.

An enjoyable experience in introducing worship is included in the six-session course. In sessions 4 and 5 a plan for developing worship around the milestones and special events of teen life is presented. A series of short worship events rather than one larger one can be developed on one or more of these themes. Such worship might also suggest some program ideas for the group.

If You Are a Young Person or Group of Young People

As a young person you may be tempted to use this book as a source of "canned" worship services. After all, you are likely to be facing a deadline. This book is not intended, however, to be merely an answer to your need but rather a spark to set off your creativity. It is hoped that you will not use anything from Part Two just the way it is but will rearrange and recombine materials so that any service becomes your own.

Part Two isn't much good without Part One, for it is here that you will learn to understand worship and develop the ability to put together a sensitive service that will lead others into an experience of worshiping God.

Ask yourself the following questions:

1. Have you wondered what this thing called worship is really about? Read Chapter 1 to deepen your understanding.

2. Are you at the beginning of your planning and in need of suggestions for the order of the service? Look in Chapters 3 and 4.

3. Do you want some original ways to use the Bible, music, the dramatic arts, or the visual arts? Read over Chapters 6 through 9.

4. Are you looking for new opportunities to plan and lead worship? Chapters 2 and 5 will be helpful.

5. Are you about to work on a service in the out-of-doors? Chapter 10 is about outdoor worship and Chapter 4 is helpful with large groups.

6. Are you trying to find some new resources for a service? Chapter 12 helps you locate resources, and Chapter 11 contains suggestions for creating your own original materials.

7. Are you trying to get your group organized? Read Chapter 13.

8. Do you need some ideas for short, informal worship in your group? Read the section for teachers of senior high classes in this User's Guide.

9. Are you responsible for leading worship? Read the last part of Chapter 4 for some suggestions.

10. Are you ready for an exciting, new, and challenging experience? Then plunge into the planning and leadership of worship.

■ ■ ■

A Six-Session Course on Worship for Young People

This six-session course on worship is designed to help senior high students

- understand the meaning of worship

- expand their knowledge of the elements of worship

- plan some worship experiences

- explore the contents of this book

Although planned for a one-hour, formal class, parts of the course can be used with youth groups as well. If all six sessions cannot be held in a six-week period, there is a natural break between sessions 3 and 4.

Basic materials needed for this course are a newsprint pad, felt markers, tape, paper, pencils, and a room with movable chairs for small-group work.

Session 1 ■ The Object of Our Worship

Purpose: To be in touch with ideas and feelings about God and to begin to relate them to the content and concept of worship.

Relevant materials from *Youth Plan Worship,* Chapter 1.

Begin by outlining what the young people will be doing in this course and especially in this particular session. If this is a new group of young people who do not know one another, take an extra ten minutes at this time to help them get to know at least one other person. Have them divide in pairs and describe to each other "the worship experience I have had that touched me most." When the group reassembles, let them simply call out the place where these experiences occurred. Note to the group the variety of places and experiences.

Ask the group to prepare for a fantasy experience by settling down. Use words similar to these, speaking slowly and in a relaxed manner. Pause every now and then.

We are going to have a fantasy experience and then talk about it. I want you to get comfortable and relaxed. Wiggle around in your chair until you are comfortable or else sit on the floor. Some people like to hold their hands on their lap palms up to relax. You will want to put both feet on the floor if you are sitting in a chair. Otherwise your foot can fall asleep. Take off your jacket if you need to so you are not too warm or too cold. Now close your eyes.

Think for a minute about your breathing. Breathe in very slowly and then breathe out. Think "in" and then think "out." Again. Again. Try to breathe through your nose if you can. Think about your feet. Move them just a little bit and then relax them. Now think about your legs and move them. Then relax them and let them go. (Move up body mentioning parts and then help the participants relax that part of their body.)

Now let a sense of peace and relaxation take over. We're going to take our minds and imaginations some place. Right now pretend you are up on a hill all alone, just enjoying yourself. The weather is perfect—whatever is perfect for you. The view is spectacular. Look around you and enjoy it. (Pause and give them time to get there.)

Slowly you become aware of the fact that you are not alone. Up here on the hill with you is another presence. Something—someone—is here with you. Suddenly you become aware that God is with you on the hill. Maybe you can picture God in your mind—or maybe just hear sounds—or maybe just feel a presence. Whatever it is for you, you are in the presence of God. Think about how you feel. For a little while just feel yourself in the presence of God. (Pause.) Now somehow acknowledge to God that you know God is there. Will you do anything? Say anything? Whatever fits for you. Is there something you want to ask God? What do you want from God? (Pause and give them time to do this.)

Now you are becoming aware of the fact that you and God are going to have to part. How will you express your "good-bye" to God? How do you think God will express it to you? Just as earlier you became aware of God's presence, now you are aware that you are alone again. *(Pause.)* You are on that special hill and alone.

Spend a moment with your aloneness. Now get up from where you are and start to walk down the hill toward *(name of your church)*. You can walk slowly or rapidly, whatever fits your mood at this point, but come on down from the hill and find *(name of church)*. Come in the front door *(talk them through the route to your room)* and find your seat here in this room. Feel that seat with your own body. Become aware of the fact that you are sitting in this room and begin to move yourself in that chair.

I'm going to count from five to one and as I do that, begin to feel more and more in this room. Five, four, become aware of your hands and feet and your body. Three, become aware of your face. Two, become aware of your eyes and open them. One, you are back here in this room, eyes open.

* * *

Have people relax quietly for a minute and then find one other person to share their experience with. Ask the pairs to scatter themselves around the room, if possible, to make it easier to talk. Have each participant tell that other person what his or her God was like. Have each tell what it felt like to be in the presence of God.

Reassemble the group. On a newsprint pad make a list of the characteristics of God that people experienced. Make another list of the feelings people had or wanted to express to God in the fantasy.

Using Chapter 1 as a guide, present the concept of worship as "worth-ship" and the way we express our concepts and feelings about God in that worship.

Prepare the class to work in small groups of three or four people. Tell them that in two weeks, God is going to come to this class and they need to plan for that time with God. Small groups will begin their work this week and complete it next week. They should take some notes so as not to forget their ideas. Have ready the following questions on newsprint:

How will we welcome God?
How will we express our feelings to God?
What do we want to happen during the time God is present?
How will we say good-bye to God?

In small groups they are to answer these questions as a way of getting started.

Bring the whole group together again and let each small group report briefly their ideas. Put the ideas on newsprint to use again next session. Suggest that members of the group think about additional possibilities during the week.

End by asking the group to sit quietly again and remember the moments they spent with God in their fantasy. Close with a simple "Amen."

Session 2 ■ The Content of Worship

Purpose: To use feelings about God to develop a simple worship experience and compare it with more traditional orders of worship.

Relevant materials from *Youth Plan Worship:* Chapter 3. Make copies of the orders of service in Chapter 3 unless you have several copies of the book to use in class.

Other resources needed: Copies of your worship bulletin on a typical Sunday or, if you do not use a bulletin, a typical order of service for your church.

Begin by reviewing what happened last time the group was together. Let those who were present describe the session to those who were absent. Review the newsprint listing the feelings people had or wanted to express to God. Add to that list other possible feelings about God.

Ask the group to stand in pairs around the room with as much space between pairs as possible. Use "statues" to help them work on how to express these feelings bodily and with words. Explain to the group that one partner will be the statue builder and the other will be the building material. Let the pairs choose who will take which role to begin with. Tell them that you will call out a feeling and the statue builder is to move the statue into a posture that expresses that feeling. Act this out with someone in the room. This device will both put the participants in touch with what they did last week and help raise some ideas for small-group work.

Begin by calling out one of the feelings from the newsprint list and give the pairs time to build their statues. Invite people to look around (statues may move their eyes only) and see what others have done. Have the pairs switch roles and try another feeling.

Now suggest that the pairs collaborate to plan a sentence that will be spoken along with the posture to illustrate this feeling in relation to God. Call out another one of the feelings on your list. After it is worked out, give each pair a chance to demonstrate. Try this with the remaining feelings, and in discussion note where these postures and words are similar to those we use in our worship.

Gather the whole group together and prepare to work again in small groups planning for God's visit to the class next week. Keep the same groups as last time, integrating new people into existing groups wherever possible. The assignment this time is to plan the sequence of events for God's visit in as much detail as possible. All the events should express their feelings *about God to God*. As a starting point for this week's work, review the ideas that the groups suggested last week. Ask for additional suggestions people may have thought of during the week. If you have the space, let each small group use newsprint to record their work to report to the whole class.

While the small groups are working, walk around and sit in on them. You may have to help them understand the project if they go off the track. Help them avoid arguments such as whether God walks in through the door or oozes in under it, and focus them on expressing their feelings *about God to God*.

Reassemble the group and let small groups report. If they did not use newsprint themselves, record their reports briefly on newsprint, making clear the order in which they placed items. If there are only two or three groups, it is interesting to make columns on the newsprint and record the reports in parallel columns for comparison.

Hand out copies of the orders of worship from Chapter 3 and copies of your own order of worship. Ask the group to look for similarities and differences between the materials they created and these orders of worship. Using the materials they have read in Chapter 3 about the flow of worship, try to help the young people see how the order of a worship service parallels their feelings about God or how it is discontinuous with it. What is the value of using a specific sequence?

Choose some people who would be willing to prepare to lead the class in one of the experiences designed by a small group. You may need to meet with them between sessions. Assign Chapters 6, 7, 8, and 9 to four different young people for reading and reporting at the next session.

End with a part of the small-group work just created. Put away the newsprint about God and feelings from sessions 1 and 2. After the worship course, you can have a fine discussion on what or who is God based on this material.

Session 3 ■ Worship With More Than Words

Purpose: To experience the worship plans made the previous session. To expand the possible approaches to worship for future planning.

Relevant materials from Youth Plan Worship: Chapters 6, 7, 8, and 9, which individuals should have read and be ready to report on.

Review what the group has been doing for those who have been absent and explain what is to happen in this session.

Let the group who were chosen lead the entire class in their planned experience of a visit from God. Spend enough time with this so that people can participate fully in the experience.

Let people form pairs and discuss the experience with their partner. Ask them in what way this ressembled other worship services they have experienced. In what ways did it differ?

Reassemble the group and let each participant affirm what was best about the experience to the whole group.

Ask the young people who were to read Chapters 6, 7, 8, and 9 to report. Since some people learn better by seeing and others by hearing, put key words on newsprint as the young people are speaking.

Make a list on newsprint of "ideas we would like to try in the future." One of the best ways to do this is to brainstorm. This means that anyone can give an idea, even if it conflicts with previous ideas. All ideas are accepted without challenge or discussion, and people are encouraged to build on other ideas. This will produce a list of worship ideas for future planning both during the course and later on. This list should be saved as a reference piece and will be used in session 5.

Session 4 ■ Inventing Our Own Ceremonies, Part A

Purpose: To understand the place of rites and rituals in the lives of young people and to begin to relate these experiences to the church and worship.

Relevant materials from *Youth Plan Worship:* Chapter 5.

Other resources needed: If possible, duplicate copies of "Invent a Ceremony" (below) for all members of the class. If not, write the steps on newsprint to post where the whole group can see it during their work time.

Begin by talking about the rituals people went through before they came to class today. Make a list on newsprint. In what way are the rituals different on weekends and weekdays?

Explain that religious rites and rituals are also part of the worship experience. We repeat the experience over and over. In Christian worship we also design some ceremonies to celebrate certain events and life passages. These ceremonies usually use some visible and tangible sign of God's love and care for us. They also express our feeling toward God at that moment in our lives.

Let the group name some ceremonies such as baptism, marriage, or a funeral and identify the signs and symbols used as well as the feelings toward God expressed. Help the group make a newsprint list of significant events and life passages that teenagers experience.

Divide the class into small groups of from three to four people. Each group is to choose one of the events or life passages and "Invent a Ceremony." Give each group newsprint and markers for their work.

Give out previously duplicated sheets or post on newsprint the following questions:

Invent a Ceremony

Your goal is to produce an order or sequence for a ceremony for an event or life passage of a teenager. Here are some questions to help you think it through.

Where should the ceremony be held?
What visible, tangible signs or symbols will you use?
What scriptures or other readings are appropriate?
What should be contained in the prayer? Is there something to be thankful for? Something to ask for?
What is the sequence of the ceremony? What comes first, what next, and what last?
Write out a sequential order for the ceremony.

While the small groups are meeting, move around from group to group to make sure they understand what they are to do.

Call the whole class together and let groups report and explain the plans they have made. Remind them that they will be working on these ceremonies further next week.

Assign three people to read Chapters 2, 4, and 10, one chapter apiece, before the next meeting. They might also look through Part Two in search of materials appropriate to any of the ceremonies being invented.

Close with a simple ceremony appropriate to your group. Perhaps you customarily say a benediction standing in a circle or have some other type of ceremony. If needed, invent something yourself.

Session 5 ■ Inventing Our Own Ceremonies, Part B

Purpose: To continue work on developing ceremonies appropriate to teenagers. To consider the place and setting for worship and how it influences the service.

Relevant materials from *Youth Plan Worship:* Chapters 2, 4, and 10 and Part Two.

Begin by outlining the class session, reminding the young people of the ceremonies they began last week. If anyone was absent, let some members of the class bring him or her up to date.

Set up a fishbowl discussion on "Where is the best place to worship God?" Let the three people who read Chapters 2, 4, and 10 during the week sit in a little circle in the center. They are to hold the discussion while the others listen in without comment. They should be encouraged to use what they have learned from their reading to buttress their point of view.

After five to ten minutes, let the three insiders join the outside circle and let everyone enter the discussion. Draw the discussion to a close by making lists of the advantages and disadvantages of worship in the church building, the classroom, the out-of-doors, and whatever other place you wish to include.

Let the person who reviewed Part Two report on ideas and resources that might be helpful in the ceremonies being worked on.

Post the ideas brainstormed in session 3 along with the work done on inventing ceremonies from the last session. Allow the whole group to give some ideas to each small group before sending the small groups back to complete their work. If there are new people, try to integrate them into existing groups. Circulate and help as needed.

Re-gather the class and let each small group report on their completed ceremony. Choose a portion of one ceremony to use as your closing worship moment.

Session 6 ■ Planning a Worship Service

Purpose: To plan a worship service or portion of a service that can be used with another group or the whole congregation. To relate one of the ceremonies to the broader experience of worship.

Relevant materials from *Youth Plan Worship:* Chapters 11 and 12.

Other resources needed: Orders of worship from session 2, Bibles, a concordance, and hymnals.

Post the completed ceremonies from the previous session. Affirm the various ceremonies created and help the group choose one of them to expand further into a larger service.

Discuss how the ideas would fit into your Sunday morning service (perhaps on Youth Sunday) or plan a time, place, and a group with whom you will share a service on the theme chosen. Chapter 2 has suggestions for some times and places. Refer back to the orders of worship used in session 2 and the list of ideas created in session 3 and set up a basic design for the worship service.

Some questions to discuss are the following:

Using the ceremony as a guide, what might be the broader theme of the worship service?

Will the plans fit into the service order used every Sunday or are there ways in which it should be changed?

If the previously invented ceremony or part of it is to be used the way it is, where in the service does it best fit?

What other parts of the service will be influenced by the theme
   suggested by the ceremony?
Are there creative ways to use music, art, drama, and reading that
   will enhance the worship and coordinate with the theme?
Is there a balance so that the worship service is not too strange for
   the people attending it?

In preparation for work in small groups actually preparing parts of
the service, share briefly some ideas from Chapter 11 on preparing
original materials. Especially focus on the creation of prayers and the
various kinds of prayers. Make a newsprint list of words that come to
mind when you think of the ceremony and theme. These can be used in
writing prayers and other parts of the service.

Divide into working groups according to interest and begin either
creating parts of the service or choosing materials already available.
Some people need to choose hymns by using the index in the hymnal
(see Chapter 12); others need to write prayers and litanies. If there is to
be a sermon or meditation, it can be outlined, and other parts of the
service will need to be worked on.

When the working groups return together, have them share those
parts of the service they have created. Appoint a small group to work
with you, the teacher, in following up on the when and where of the
service and in making final plans.

Celebrate the weeks of work on worship by using a portion of what
the class have created to end the session.

PART ONE

Planning for Worship

The chapters in Part One have been designed to help young people and their leaders understand the meaning of worship and the many elements that go into it. It is important to read it before turning to Part Two on resources. The two kinds of materials — knowledge about worship and worship materials themselves — should be kept in balance.

The Why of Worship

It is often said that worship is a drama. If that is so, who do you think the actors are and who is the audience? Where does the basic script come from? Before reading the chapter, write down what you think worship really is.

"Who's got worship tonight?" Susan began.

"Guess I have," Al said, a bit tentatively.

"But, but . . ." Eleven pairs of eyes turned toward Liz. "I thought Ruth Ann . . . What I mean is, Ruth Ann thought she was supposed to lead worship tonight. She's done a lot of work on a service."

"Well, yes, I have," Ruth Ann admitted in response to several inquiring glances. "I guess I misunderstood."

"Does anyone know for sure?" Susan asked. "Mr. Edwins, do you know?"

The adult adviser shook his head. "It looks to me as though this group had better get itself organized," he added, noting concern on the faces around him.

* * *

Cupcakes were the order of the day as the Cooper twins, Bill and Tom, played host to Kris and Leona, who had come in after school to work on planning the Youth Sunday service.

"Here's a hymn to sing," Bill said, sitting with a hymnal in one hand and a chocolate cupcake in the other. "I always like 'Blest Be the Tie That Binds.' "

"Sure, you always like it. We sing it every time you are part of the planning committee. Wouldn't it be better to get some variety into this service?" counseled Kris.

Reluctantly Bill agreed, then just as abruptly called out, "Number 20 would be good — 'The Church's One Foundation.' "

This time Leona and Tom both spoke at once. "No, it wouldn't. This service is supposed to be on ecology. Remember?"

Finally Bill caught on. Slamming the hymnbook closed, he conceded, "Well, maybe we had better plan out the rest of the service first!"

* * *

Four young people had just finished leading a worship service in the nursing home and were letting off steam as they drove away.

"Where did you find that perfect meditation?" George asked Pat. "It fitted the worship service to a T."

"Why," Pat answered, "one night at supper I mentioned that I had the meditation for the nursing home service this week. Dad remembered something he had seen in the magazine section of Sunday's paper that was right in line with the subject of world peace. 'That's great,' I said, 'Why couldn't it be in tonight's paper? Mother hasn't thrown that out yet!'

"Dad just looked at me and said, 'Patricia, that's what libraries are for. You go down after supper and ask for last Sunday's paper. You'll find the article I'm talking about.'

"That was it. Dad was right. I found it!"

The group liked Bob's prayer, too. "It was so beautiful," Eleanor said. "It sounded as if it came right out of the Bible. Did it?"

"It came from a book in the pastor's library," Bob said. "It's called The Book of Common Prayer." He held it up for the group to see. "I asked Dr. Stewart if she could help me find a prayer on world peace. She took this book down from one of her shelves and showed me how to look up prayers in it. She let me bring it along to show you. I think we ought to have a copy in the church library."

"And, let's be sure to put Pat's meditation in the worship file," added Eleanor.

* * *

Do these stories have a familiar sound? Undoubtedly you could add many more from the experiences of your own youth group, for worship is one of the activities that distinguishes your church group from school and social clubs.

But no matter whether your group worships regularly as a part of its meetings or only occasionally at retreats and special events, it is true that few young people have come to an understanding of worship and its meaning. They often go through a worship service perfunctorily, with little or no sense of its purpose, or when asked to lead, they have little idea where to begin. Planning and leading worship well are steps toward integrating worship more fully into one's life and into a group's life. To begin, it is important to understand something of the meaning of worship, especially corporate or group worship.

Worship is often defined as "response to God." It is the way in which Christians show appreciation for God's power and greatness and for God's presence in their lives. The word worship itself means "worth-ship" and stands for devotion to that which we believe has worth to us. We talk of people worshiping money or a person they love. Christian worship celebrates the fact that God, as shown to us by Jesus Christ, is that which is most worthy in our lives. God has ultimate worth in our lives and so we worship God.

There are, of course, personal ways of worshiping God, and when we meditate, pray, or read devotional materials alone we are engaging in personal worship. But group worship, or corporate worship as it is sometimes called, is somewhat different, for it takes into account not only ourselves and God but our relationships to one another. Corporate worship is the community of faith coming together and responding to God *together* both as individuals and as a group. It means we pay attention to the presence of other people as well as the presence of God.

In its simplest form, worship includes three main movements: our approach to God, God's approach to us, and our response to God in dedication or service.

We begin by turning our thoughts to God individually and as a group, sometimes with a sense of gathering and always with a form of adoration or praise. Through scripture or meditation, dance, music, silence, or whatever, we listen for God's word to us.

The test of our experience comes in the third step. If we have felt a sense of community with God, we feel a fresh desire to work in the direction in which God leads us. So in a spirit of commitment we affirm our faith or offer ourselves to God's service.

Always God is the center of our worship and the person on whom we focus our worship. If worship is a drama, it is God who is the audience and we who are the actors. The Bible and our church traditions give us the basis of a script and the means by which the whole group or congregation can be brought together in an act of worship.

The When of Worship

All of us have experienced corporate worship with a congregation. Make a list of other times when you have been a part of group worship. Have there been times in your life when you wished a group would include a worship service, even in a simple form? When would it have been appropriate? What do you think kept the group from making such plans?

In the not too distant past, many youth groups and high school church school classes have included regular worship services in their schedules. With the emphasis on worship as a whole community of faith in the last fifteen to twenty years, church schools have often dropped the practice. Youth fellowships, too, have sometimes moved away from the weekly worship service. One way of beginning to include times of worship again is to have a closing fellowship circle. The group could sing a familiar hymn or a song such as "Kum Bah Yah" and say a short prayer. Some groups like to include silence for people to add their own prayers.

Retreats form another setting in which the group can begin to plan worship experiences for themselves. Vespers around a fireplace or campfire in the early evening or a midnight communion service are popular formats and easy ways to begin. The changed setting of a trip away from the church leaves people more open to new experiences.

Once your group has some experience with worship, you may want to try other occasions and formats. The User's Guide has some suggestions for worship moments in a class, which could also be adapted for youth groups.

Assisting in Congregational Worship

Sometimes the first opportunity for a leadership role in worship occurs in the Sunday morning service. Young people assist in such roles as acolyte, usher, member of the choir, and scripture reader. Training should be provided by the church. If not, young people should take the lead in requesting a chance to practice before reading or speaking in front of the whole congregation.

New Opportunities for Leadership

Youth Sunday services have been with us for a long time, but they seem to be having a revival recently. They provide an opportunity for the youth of a church to plan and lead the entire Sunday morning service for the congregation. In such planning the following questions ought to be considered: Should you follow your church's usual order of worship or change it? Are Youth Sundays for young people or for adults that come? What do young people most want to share with adults at this time? Are there some alternatives to the traditional sermon that would be effective ways of communicating ideas?

Easter sunrise services led by youth are another old tradition being revived in many places. They are most effective outdoors, although it is important to have an indoor place available in case of rain. One person should be in charge of making the indoor-or-outdoor decision and communicating it to those leading and attending the service. If an outdoor service is to be held in a public park or other public place, someone must be sure to obtain permission well in advance, since some public places have rules that affect the kind of service you can hold. After the service some groups furnish a tailgate breakfast of fruit juice, coffee, and doughnuts. Be sure to check Chapter 10 "Worship in the Out-of-Doors" for ideas.

Young people who want to increase the number of opportunities to plan and lead worship might volunteer to plan for a local nursing home or a group of younger children in the church school. Worship for an intergenerational event, such as an Advent workshop, could be tried. Services for special occasions not otherwise celebrated in a particular church offer another new opportunity. Some examples are a Watch Night service on New Year's Eve, a Shrove Tuesday pancake supper ending in a service to begin Lent, the hanging of the greens early in Advent or their "taking down" on Epiphany with an appropriate service, a Maundy Thursday service including a drama based on the Last Supper, a Good Friday service of readings and recorded music.

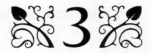

3

Planning Meaningful Worship

Obtain a copy of a recent bulletin for your church or another church's worship. Look up the hymns, scriptures, and readings. See if you can figure out the theme. Do the scripture readings and the hymns go together in any way? Were the hymns chosen for their place in the flow of the service? Compare the order of the service with some of the orders suggested in this chapter.

The whole purpose of this book is to help you plan meaningful worship, but this chapter deals with some specific areas that need to be considered early on in your work—the choice of a theme, the use of language, and the flow of worship itself.

Using a Theme

As important as it is for the elements of a congregational worship service to fit together on Sunday morning, it is even more critical that those of a short service or service for a special occasion come together through the use of a theme. Ideas for a theme come from many places. On an ordinary Sunday, they can come from the lectionary (a group of scripture readings planned for each Sunday and holiday of the church year). Sometimes the theme comes from the place the Sunday occupies in the church year. There is an explanation of the church year in Chapter 5 along with other emphases often used in churches.

The theme of your own youth-group program or church school curriculum is a good starting point for worship in your own group. In addition to the life of your own group, experiences common to the life of a teenager can provide ideas for worship. Session 4 of the worship course in the User's Guide deals with developing worship from such life experiences.

Another source of ideas for themes is the point at which the worship comes in the life of the group itself. Worship at the beginning of a conference or retreat can focus on the coming together of the group; at the end it can include the dedication of one's life and/or a sense of ending.

The services included in Part Two of this book are built around themes as indicated by the title of the service or meditation. Hymns, scriptures, and other materials that will carry the theme forward are suggested.

Inclusive Language

As high school young people begin studying languages other than English, they discover the fact that words form our way of looking at the world. We don't control our language as much as our language gives us ideas and categories that control us. The English language has been ambiguous in the way in which the words man and he have been used. It has used masculine words specifically to mean male persons and more generally to mean all people.

Recently people have become aware that using masculine words when they mean both women and men causes several problems. First, it is confusing because we are not sure if only males or all people is meant. Second, because words control the way we look at things, the use of masculine words for people in general means that we subconsciously leave out women or at the least think of males as representative of all people. For these reasons many people are concerned that in worship, of all places, we use language that includes everyone. The use of only inclusive language in many church publications has proved that it does not need to be awkward but requires us to think a bit differently about our world when we speak and write.

In an effort to help people think in less limited ways about God, language for God has been changing also. Since God is neither male nor female, some people are avoiding the use of masculine or feminine words for God, and others are using both kinds of words. Many people are seeking to expand and enlarge our ideas of God and make more use of neutral words such as "Sustainer," "Gracious God," and "Creator." As you plan your worship services, you will need to take into account the importance of including all people in the language you use.

Planning an Order of Worship

A worship service is more than a collection of hymns, prayers, Bible readings, and other materials. Worship needs to go somewhere, to flow toward a goal and to move smoothly from beginning to end. It would, of course, be monotonous to sing all the hymns at once, pray all the prayers together, and then listen to all the speaking parts. But, more than that, it would not allow for the rhythm mentioned in Chapter 1 of our approach to God, God's approach to us, and our response to God. A good order of worship keeps the worshiper from getting lost and offers opportunities to listen, see, and learn, and to respond in singing, speaking, or moving.

One traditional order of worship comes from Isaiah 6:1–8. The experience described is that of the Old Testament prophet Isaiah, who was saddened at the death of King Uzziah.

In the first verses of the passage "I saw the Lord, . . . high and lifted up [6:1a]" and later in the words "Holy, holy, holy is the Lord of hosts; the whole earth is full of his glory [6:3b]," we find the ancient counterpart to a call to worship and hymn of praise.

In verses 5 to 7, Isaiah becomes conscious of being in the presence of God and realizes how unworthy of God's love he is. He says, "Woe to me! For I am lost; . . . my eyes have seen . . . the Lord!" When Isaiah hears the words "Your guilt is taken away, and your sin forgiven," he receives God's forgiveness just as we do in our prayer of confession and assurance of pardon.

Then the prophet heard the voice of God saying, "Whom shall I send, and who will go for us?" In our own worship we receive God's promptings for our lives through the readings from the Bible, the prayers, drama, and so on. Finally, even as Isaiah answered, "Here I am! Send me," so we respond to God in our prayers, our offering, our hymns of dedication, and other such acts. A worship service ordered around the Isaiah 6 passage might look like this:

Prelude
Call to Worship
Hymn of Praise
Prayer of Confession
Assurance of Forgiveness
Scripture Reading
Meditation or other Reflection
Prayer
Offering
Hymn of Dedication
Benediction

Another order of worship comes from the traditions of the Episcopal Church.

THE PEOPLE AND PRIEST:

gather in the Lord's name
proclaim and respond to the word of God
(The proclamation and response may include, in addition to a reading from the Gospel, other readings, song, talk, dance, instrumental music, other art forms, silence.)
pray for the world and the church
exchange the peace
prepare the table
make eucharist
break the bread
share the gifts of God

A very simple order of service used by groups could simply include the following:

Call to Worship
Hymn
Scripture Reading
Response to scripture in the form of meditation, music, discussion, dance, etc.
Prayer
Benediction

In the *Worshipbook* (Philadelphia: Westminster Press, 1970, p. 23) a traditional order of service appears, which might be adaptable for your use. Compare it with the previous orders of service.

Call to Worship	Creed
Hymn of Praise	Prayer of the People
Confession of Sin	The Peace
Declaration of Pardon	Offering
Response	Prayer of Thanksgiving
Prayer for Illumination	The Lord's Prayer
Old Testament Lesson	Hymn
New Testament Lesson(s)	Charge
Sermon	Benediction

4

Providing an Atmosphere for Worship

Complete the following sentences:
  I worship best when . . .
  What keeps me from feeling worshipful is . . .
  The best kind of worship leader is one who . . .

To create an appropriate atmosphere for worship is every bit as important as selecting the right hymns or preparing an inspiring prayer or meditation. Protestant worship has tended to be centered on words, and too often the sensory experiences of the eye, movements and actions, and the surrounding environment has been ignored. In the last thirty years or so, what is called the liturgical renewal movement has helped everyone become more aware of the place, the mood, the sense of ceremony, and the role of the leader.

A Place for Worship

It is entirely possible to worship in a room bare of religious symbols of any kind. The most exalted moments of worship that some groups will ever know have frequently occurred in the midst of a serious discussion, when the setting was a completely secondary consideration. The Pilgrims made their meeting houses as plain as possible in order to purify their worship of the pomp and ceremony of the Church of England, and to this day the Quakers believe that God can be approached best when the mind is free from distractions of ornament in the surroundings.

Most people, however, have not trained themselves to worship in such austere settings and appreciate the opportunity to worship in an atmosphere that speaks to them of the presence of the Holy Spirit. On the one hand, though God is present as much in one room as another, to have a place set aside for worship sometimes seems more conducive to the right frame of mind. The very act of going into another room for worship helps many people to enter into God's gates with thanksgiving and into God's courts with praise.

On the other hand, some acts of worship belong in the particular work and study area of a group. If the members have a real sense of themselves as a group and if the worship is closely related to the group's work, then remaining in the work setting may add a special dimension. The work setting may also allow worship to occur at several times during a session rather than in one big service.

If the group is small or of moderate size, and if the room permits, it is desirable to have the chairs arranged in a semicircle so that everyone can see the leaders. If the group is too large for a one-row semicircle, the chairs may be set in a semicircle two or three rows deep. Except on special occasions it is not a good idea for a smallish group to go into the church sanctuary for worship. A relatively small group finds itself lost in such a space, and singing and responsive reading are difficult to carry on effectively.

Only if the group is very large or if permanent pews are provided, should theater-style seating be considered. When such seating is used, chairs should be arranged with one or more aisles between sections for ease in reaching the seats. Side aisles are often better than a center aisle unless audiovisual material is to be projected. The number of chairs set up should approximate closely the number of persons expected with a few extra saved in the rear for latecomers. A large number of vacant chairs encourages a scattering of the group throughout the room. It is important, too, that chairs be set up in advance of the service so that worshipers feel welcome when they arrive.

Setting the Mood

Worship services have many different kinds of moods, ranging from peaceful and meditative to colorful and joyous to somber and quiet. The specific content of the service is, of course, the main determinant of the mood, but the physical setting can enhance or conflict with the content. First decide on what feelings will be evoked by the theme and then look at your setting to see what needs to be done. What is permanent and what is changeable in the room? Will a lighting change help? A change in seating arrangement? Special decorations?

Some focus of attention, or worship center, is needed. In Protestant sanctuaries, such a focus is usually provided by a communion table or altar. In other settings, a less formal piece of furniture such as a table may be used, although a banner, projected slide, or other center of attention is also appropriate. If a table is used, it may hold a Bible, flowers, a picture, or other symbolic objects related to the service. Whatever is put on the table should be arranged as artistically as possible, avoiding a cluttered look.

A simple triptych can be constructed from three pieces of fiberboard hinged together and painted tan on one side and dark blue or green on the other. This can be placed at the rear of a table to make an effective background for symbols, pictures, or other objects used in the worship for the day.

The room itself can be decorated to aid the worship mood. Banners, streamers, balloons, mobiles, and other art work can be used effectively if chosen with care and coordinated with the theme. In addition, thought should be given to how people will enter the room, including the use of music and processions as well as the absence or presence of ushers. Rehearsals of songs or readings are better done in another setting or before the Call to Worship.

For groups that are staying in the same place for worship as for work or study, it is especially important to pay attention to the transition. Some groups find it helpful to "center down" through music, silence, or guided meditation at the very beginning. Often it is helpful deliberately to put away study materials or to move the chairs to a slightly different location.

Leaders of Worship

More important than external arrangements in creating an atmosphere of worship is the way in which the leader conducts the service. The following are important guidelines for all worship leaders:

1. Prepare carefully in advance.
2. Arrange the worship setting ahead of time.
3. Understand the meaning of everything you will read aloud.
4. Practice beforehand reading the materials you have chosen.
5. Keep a written order of worship in front of you at all times, including the words to such well-known parts of the service as the Lord's Prayer. (Many ministers make a practice of doing this to guard against the temporary lapses of memory to which we all are subject.)
6. Be sure that the musicians know the hymns and other musical selections and have had opportunity to practice them. Instruments should be in tune.

7. Sit near the front of the room, if no special chair is provided for leaders.
8. Speak loudly enough to be heard and clearly and slowly enough to be understood.
9. Participate in the service yourself. Leading worship is more than announcing hymn numbers and pages in books.
10. Don't use special inflections or tones in your voice during prayers. (This is known jokingly as a "holy tone" or a stained-glass voice.)
11. Don't make extemporaneous speeches. Carefully planned meditations may be given from an outline, but a complete lack of preparation results in a disorganized message.
12. Don't light candles unceremoniously.
13. Don't show off.
14. Don't begin the service until you are sure that all arrangements have been completed and that those who are participating know what their responsibilities are.
15. Finally, pray for God's guidance as you prepare to lead others in worship.

Events for Very Large Groups

Worship events at camps and conferences, for clusters of churches and regional and national youth events, need planners just as local worship does. Overall themes are usually established well in advance. Worship leaders may find themselves working many months prior to the service. In addition to what has already been said in this chapter, some special things should be taken into account for large gatherings.

1. Use the space to advantage. At least one person from the planning group should try to visit the space for worship and describe it to the others. Don't assume the group needs to sit in rows like pews unless that is what you really want. Check the acoustics and the sight lines ahead of time to be sure your plans make the best use of the space.
2. Think big. Banners need to be large, or else use a large number of banners; processionals need large numbers of people. Small objects on the altar or communion table can seem lost unless they are handled with large motions or framed with large blocks of color.
3. Pay particular attention to the music. Musical accompaniment should be firm and well paced. If it lags, the congregation itself

may well start singing at a faster tempo. Music with repetitious lines or refrains works especially well with large groups.

4. Be clear about how you want the congregation to move. Standing and sitting should be clearly indicated by the worship leader. Clear and explicit directions should be given for any other movements, especially if worshipers are to leave their seats. Think through in advance such problems as congestion in the aisles.

5. Seriously consider using a worship bulletin. Unless hymnals are easily available and contain all the hymns you wish to use, bulletins allow for a greater choice in music. They also allow you to use new litanies or prayers, and they help the group to know what is coming next in the service.

The Church Year and the Calendar Year

Listed below are the major seasons and days of the church year. Try to put them in order and then check with the chapter to see if you are correct. A clue: Begin with Advent.

Advent

Ash Wednesday

Christmas Eve

Christmas Day

Easter

Epiphany

Good Friday

Lent

Maundy Thursday

Palm Sunday

Pentecost

Shrove Tuesday

"Variety is the spice of life," according to the poet, and who does not enjoy the variety added to daily living by the changing seasons and special festival days of the calendar year? Although the American civil calendar dates this era from the birth of Christ, the church measures time by means of a calendar of its own, with special seasons and festivals. In this calendar, every Sunday, as well as some weekdays, has a special name. Seasons of the church year, or the Christian year, are part of a cycle by which the church reviews annually the life, ministry, death, and resurrection of Jesus; the growth of the church; and the meaning of Jesus' message.

Some denominations follow the church year more closely than others, although there is a widespread, growing interest in emphasizing its meanings. In addition, interdenominational groups and almost every denomination set aside certain days and times for special emphases, such as stewardship and missions.

Days and Seasons of the Christian Year

For Protestants and Roman Catholics, the Christian year itself begins with the first Sunday in Advent rather than with the first Sunday of January. This Sunday is the one closest to November 30 and begins a four-Sunday season of anticipating the coming of Christ. Churches typically light purple candles to mark off the weeks and a single, white Christ candle on Christmas Eve or Christmas Day. The feeling of the season is usually one of expectation or waiting, and many churches delay singing Christmas carols until Christmas itself.

Christmas Eve inaugurates the new season of Christmastide, which lasts through January 5. The Epiphany season, symbolizing the coming of Jesus as the light of the world, begins on January 6. This day is sometimes called Twelfth Night since it comes twelve days after Christmas. It is traditionally the time of the coming of the Wise Men and is observed often as the time to take down the decorations, put away the crêche, and burn the Christmas tree. During Epiphany season the mission of the church in the world is sometimes the emphasis in services.

Epiphany ends on Shrove Tuesday, the day before Ash Wednesday. Celebrations on Shrove Tuesday, known in some non-English-speaking countries as Mardi Gras or Fastnacht, are very festive. The Lenten season then begins on Ash Wednesday, the fortieth weekday before Easter, with an emphasis on humility, penitence, and spiritual renewal. Ash Wednesday services often include people's receiving ashes on their foreheads as an act of confession and a sign of mortality.

Passion Sunday, or Palm Sunday, the Sunday before Easter, introduces Holy Week, commemorating Christ's passion. This is a good opportunity for a procession and a dramatic ceremony reminding people of Christ's triumphal entry into Jerusalem. Thursday of that week is known as Maundy Thursday, the night on which the Lord's Supper was instituted. It can be celebrated with a play about Jesus and perhaps a supper and communion service. Friday is Good Friday, the day of the crucifixion. Worship services on this solemn day often include much silence and prayer. An "order for Tenebrae" (Latin for "shadows") is used on either of these nights, and it includes scripture reading and the extinguishing of candles. Late on Saturday evening some churches are beginning to use an Easter Vigil service, in which the light is rekindled and the very beginning of Easter Day is celebrated.

Easter, commemorating Christ's resurrection, is the great festival of the church year, ushering in a season of fifty days known as Eastertide. It concludes with Pentecost, the traditional anniversary of the descent of the Holy Spirit upon the disciples gathered in Jerusalem and the birthday of the church. Flames, doves, wind, and the color red are used in the service. Often this is a time of great celebration and fun. Many churches choose Pentecost for their service of confirmation.

The Sunday following Pentecost is known as Trinity Sunday, and it ushers in the final season of the church year. This is variously known as Trinity season, Pentecost season, or Kingdomtide, and the emphasis is usually on Christ's presence among the people.

In addition to the specific seasons of the church year and special days such as Christmas, churches often recognize special days in the civil year. Thanksgiving Day in particular has been observed in many communities with interfaith services. Memorial Day, Independence Day, and Martin Luther King, Jr.'s birthday are observed with worship services in some areas of the country.

Church school groups and youth fellowships can take advantage of the various calendar seasons and dates in planning their own worship. In addition, they can use the calendar to find opportunities to lead the congregation or an intergenerational group in worship.

A Calendar of Possibilities follows. In Part Two, "A Calendar of Resources and Index" includes a guide to appropriate sections of the book to help you plan your service.

A Calendar of Possibilities

Advent — The season from the Sunday nearest November 30 to
    Christmas Eve
St. Nicholas Day — December 6
Human Rights Day — December 10
St. Lucia Day — December 13
Christmas Eve — December 24
Christmas Day — December 25
Watch Night (New Year's Eve) — December 31
New Year's Day — January 1
Epiphany (Three Kings Day) — January 6
Martin Luther King, Jr.'s birthday — January 15 (celebrated on the
    third Monday in January)
Week of Prayer for Christian Unity — January 18 to 25
Boy Scout Sunday — Sunday closest to February 8
Lincoln's birthday — February 12
Washington's birthday — February 22 (Presidents' Day celebrated on
    the third Monday in February)
World Day of Prayer — First Friday in March
Girl Scout Sunday — Sunday before March 12
Shrove Tuesday (Fastnacht or Mardi Gras) — Day before Ash
    Wednesday

Ash Wednesday — Fortieth day (not including Sundays) before Easter

Lent — Season from Ash Wednesday to Easter Eve

One Great Hour of Sharing — A Sunday in Lent, varying by denomination

Earth Day — March 21

Palm Sunday — Sunday before Easter

Holy Week — Week between Palm Sunday and Easter

Maundy Thursday — Thursday of Holy Week

Good Friday — Friday of Holy Week

Eastertide — Season beginning on Easter and ending on Pentecost

Easter — The first Sunday after the full moon on or next after March 21. Check with a church calendar or dictionary for date each year.

Festival of the Christian Home (Mother's Day) — Second Sunday in May

Ascension Day — Fortieth Day of Eastertide (always a Thursday)

Pentecost (Whitsunday) — Fiftieth day of Eastertide (Seventh Sunday after Easter)

Trinity Sunday — Sunday after Pentecost

Independence Day — July 4

Labor Sunday — Sunday before Labor Day

Labor Day — First Monday in September

World Communion Sunday — First Sunday in October

Access Sunday (for the handicapped) — Second Sunday in October

World Food Day — October 16

World Order Sunday — Sunday before United Nations Day

United Nations Day — October 24

Reformation Sunday — Sunday on or before October 31

All Saints Day — November 1

Stewardship Sunday — Varies by denomination but usually in November

Bible Sunday — Third Sunday in November

Thanksgiving Sunday — Sunday before Thanksgiving

Thanksgiving — Fourth Thursday in November

Every denomination also has special days and anniversaries. If your denomination puts out a calendar, check with your pastor to look for other possibilities.

Using the Bible in Worship

Make a list of the various ways you have seen scripture used in worship services. Which way was most effective? Why? Describe a time when the method of presentation most fit in with the words being presented.

The Bible holds a key position throughout every service of worship. Not only is it customary to read a scripture lesson, but nearly every element in the service is drawn in some measure from the Bible.

Often the call to worship is a passage from the Book of Psalms, and hymns are frequently rooted in scripture. Prayers draw on the great devotional passages of the Bible, and meditations are usually based on a biblical text. The offertory sentences and the benediction generally come from either the Old or New Testament, and even the order of worship itself may follow the outline of Isaiah 6:1–8, which is the story of the prophet's vision in the Temple, as noted in Chapter 4.

Although this chapter will focus on the reading of sections of scripture, it is important to remember that scripture can be presented through other means as well. Drama and dance, clowning and mime, banners and other forms of the visual arts, as well as music and film, can be the means of including the Bible in worship. Their use is covered in other chapters.

Reading the Scriptures Aloud

Choose the Passage Carefully

Nothing mars a worship service more quickly than a scripture selection that is poorly read, unless it is not well chosen. It is not enough to let the

Bible fall open and hope to find some message on the page. Nor is it a good idea always to read one of the very familiar passages. It is far better to choose a passage that is related to the theme of the service.

If you have trouble locating an appropriate scripture selection, either because you cannot remember where it is found or because you cannot think of an appropriate passage, turn to a Bible concordance. In a concordance each principal word in the Bible is listed in alphabetical order, with book, chapter, and verse to show where it is found. An abridged concordance is often bound into the pages of a study edition of the Bible. A very large, complete concordance, too expensive for most individuals to own, may be in your church or public library or your pastor's study.

In the last ten years there has been an increased interest in the use of lectionaries, which are outlines of Bible passages appropriate to the various Sundays of the church year. A lectionary is a good place to locate appropriate scripture passages as well as to find help for planning themes especially around dates in the church year. Three-year lectionaries as well as helpful study guides have been developed by several denominations. Your pastor can help you find the lectionary in common use in your own denomination.

Learn What the Passage Means

You will be able to read the scriptures aloud effectively only if you know what you are reading about. This usually means that you will need to study the selection in its context. Look up the names of unfamiliar persons or places in a Bible dictionary to discover their place in the story as well as to learn the correct pronunciation. Additional background information on the passage can be found in a Bible commentary from your church library.

Plan the Presentation

Although we are most used to hearing a single person reading a scripture passage, this is not the only approach. Many passages can be arranged for choral reading or for two or three readers. This variation in voices gives greater depth and meaning to the reading and often casts a new light on an old passage. Passages with characters speaking to each other can be arranged dramatically with a narrator and speakers.

In addition, the entire congregation can be a part of the reading. If the words are available in pew Bibles, hymnals, or a bulletin, the congregation can read in unison or read alternating between leader and people or right side and left side. In alternating sections of scripture it is important that the material be arranged appropriately. Merely alternating verses often breaks the continuity. Congregational or group reading helps bind the group into a greater sense of community.

Since some scripture passages make little sense when read without background, plan a one- or two-sentence introduction to the reading to explain something of the context.

Read the Passage Well

Before attempting to read a scripture passage as part of a worship service, practice reading it aloud. Be careful to read according to the punctuation marks, not according to the verse numbers, since frequently a verse ends in the middle of a sentence. After you have looked up the pronunciation of strange or difficult names, practice saying these words aloud again and again until they come easily. In a day when foreign names are so much in the headlines, there is no excuse for stumbling over biblical names. Finally, read slowly and with feeling, for the Bible is a lively book that needs to be allowed to speak to lively people.

Choosing Which Version to Read

You may already own several translations of the Bible yourself and wonder which one to use. The following descriptions of the most popular versions will help you choose.

The King James Version is the old, familiar English translation made in 1611. Although many passages are very beautiful, the years have brought changes in the meanings of words, and some of the words are no longer in common use.

The Revised Standard Version is an American Protestant Bible published in 1952. It is the most common, large, pulpit Bible found in churches today. This translation retains the dignity of the King James Version, but it is much clearer to a twentieth-century reader. It is based on the most accurate scholarship of its day. An *Inclusive-Language Lectionary* based on the RSV has been developed by a committee of scholars.

The New English Bible, translated by a committee of British scholars, is a fresh new translation that departs from the style of the King James Version in favor of a completely contemporary vocabulary, idiom, style, and rhythm. It does, however, include British words, which may sound strange to an American audience.

The Jerusalem Bible is the work of Roman Catholic translators. It reflects good scholarship and contains introductory essays, extensive footnotes, tables, and maps. It is useful for study and reading aloud.

The Living Bible Paraphrased is a very readable and popular version, but it is flawed by its unreliability. The team of translators adds embellishments and interpretations as part of the text without noting them as such. It is good for rapid reading but not for study or for reading in worship.

The Amplified Bible, translated by Frances E. Siewert, uses multiple English words and phrases to suggest the range of meanings in the original Hebrew and Greek. This version is, therefore, wordy, and more useful for study than for reading aloud.

The Good News Bible (Today's English Version) is a new translation in the language of today extensively illustrated with line drawings by Annie Valloton. Although translated from the best available texts, the attempt to simplify the language means that some of the grandeur and dignity of many sections is lost.

The New International Version, one of the most recent translations, is among the best available. It is a scholarly attempt to get at the original meanings for today's readers.

Most of the translations mentioned above are likely to be available through your church or your pastor. It is always helpful to check several versions even if you are committed to read from a particular one. In addition to those listed, there are several broad paraphrases, which are useful on special occasions.

The Cotton Patch Version of Matthew and John; The Cotton Patch Version of Luke and Acts; and *The Cotton Patch Version of Paul's Epistles* by Clarence Jordan bring parts of the New Testament to life by modern paraphrase set in the southern part of the United States.

Psalms Now and *Epistles Now* by Leslie F. Brandt are not translations but attempts to put biblical concepts in modern English.

Music in Worship

What is your favorite hymn or religious song? What is there about it that appeals to you? Where did you learn it or first sing it? In what way does the place you encountered it have anything to do with why it is special to you? If you have the words handy, look them up and identify which sections are most meaningful. This chapter suggests that more theology is taught through hymn texts than through sermons. What do you think of that observation?

The main reason for singing hymns in worship is that they are a form of the service in which all members of the congregation may take part. A hymn may be a tribute to God's greatness and power, a form of prayer, or a means of responding to God's call, but the combination of words and music sung together in a large group can lift hearts to God in ways that few other things can.

Christians also sing hymns because the words carry a message. Someone has said that more theology has been learned from hymn texts than from all the sermons ever preached, for the poetry is easy to remember and often stays in the memory throughout life. Some hymn texts, however, may contain theological ideas that are not in keeping with the teachings of your denomination or may express ideas that are no longer generally supported. This is one reason why it is so important that your church or church school use a good hymnal, preferably one published by your denomination, and for you to pay attention to the words of hymns you choose.

Music in worship does not, however, need to be confined to hymns, either old or new. Many good popular or rock songs are about themes important to youth and include a message consistent with Christian theology. Certain musicians such as John Lennon and Simon and Garfunkle never seem to go out of date, and musicals such as *Godspell* and *Jesus Christ, Superstar* contain many songs worth using in worship.

Ways of Using Music Sung by the Congregation

The resource section indicates various ways of using hymns. Often a hymn may serve as a theme or focus for building a service, and several meditations on music are included. A list of hymns on each theme is also a part of the resource section.

Quite a number of new hymns and religious songs have been written over the last fifteen years and may be used in place of traditional hymns. Since their quality is uneven, it is important that you pay attention to both the music and the words in considering them for use in worship, just as you would pay attention to the content of a hymn. Since popular songs tend to come and go, this chapter will focus more on traditional hymnody, though much of what is said is broadly applicable.

Often, when the words of a hymn come from the Bible, a service may be built upon the comparison between the words of the Bible text and the words of the hymn, leading to a better appreciation of both. Another service focusing on a hymn can be built around the story of the circumstances in which the hymn was written. Still another service might be built around a series of hymns following a theme. This approach is different from a hymn sing, where the choice of music is spontaneous.

Another important use of music in worship is the singing of short responses at various points in a service: as a response to a call to worship or to a scripture reading, after a prayer or litany, or following the giving of an offering. Sometimes the refrain of a hymn or other song is used in this way — often as the response in a litany in place of a spoken response.

Almost every hymnal has a section of chants and responses from which to choose. Many of the hymns themselves have refrains that are appropriate such as:

> Rejoice, rejoice,
> Rejoice, give thanks and sing.

Other hymns that contain refrains that make excellent responses include "For the Beauty of the Earth," "God of the Earth, the Sky, the Sea," "O Come, O Come, Emmanuel," "Angels We Have Heard on High," "O Come, All Ye Faithful," "The First Noel," "We Plow the Fields and Scatter," "Thine Is the Glory," as well as some of the spirituals, such as "Lord, I Want to Be a Christian," and "Every Time I Feel the Spirit."

Recorded Music

Listening to recorded music can be appropriate at almost any point in a service of worship. Portions of popular records are usable for meditation times as well as for prelude or postlude music. Recorded music can accompany movement or slides, but care must be taken to avoid lengthy pieces and passive listening. Classical music, such as Handel's *Messiah*, can be used if the pieces are somewhat familiar to young people. Recorded music is not a substitute for group singing.

Choosing Music to Sing

Care is necessary, of course, in selecting music for worship as noted earlier. In addition, certain kinds of music fit best at given times in the service. Often the first hymn or song will be one of praise regardless of the theme of the service. Music that follows will be more in keeping with the overall theme, and a final piece often includes aspects of dedication and consecration. As churches are becoming more aware of cultural diversity, leaders are seeking out songs from a variety of ethnic groups. You might want to include some black, Hispanic, or other ethnic music on occasion.

You will need to become familiar with the indexes of your hymnal in order to do a good job in planning group worship. Most hymnals have several indexes; the one most commonly used is the "Index of First Lines." There you will find a hymn such as "America the Beautiful" listed under the first line of its text, "O beautiful for spacious skies."

The next most useful index is the "Topical Index," particularly when you are looking for a hymn appropriate for a special theme. Under "Church," for example, you will find listed such hymns as "The Church's One Foundation," "Glorious Things of Thee Are Spoken," and "I Love Thy Kingdom, Lord." Frequently by leafing through a hymnal you will come upon the hymns that pertain to a given topic grouped together on adjacent pages.

Locating Hymn Tunes

There are also indexes that list hymn tunes by their names. Each hymn tune has a name that is different from the name of the text and often indicates something of the historic uses of the hymn and even its place of origin. Most hymnals list the names of these tunes alphabetically with the numbers of all hymns sung to that tune listed opposite the name. "Adeste Fideles" is the name of the tune to which "O Come, All Ye

Faithful" and sometimes "How Firm a Foundation" are sung. Occasionally you will find that the same tune is written in a different key in each place; when this happens your pianist or accompanist can select the key best suited to the voices in your group.

There is also a metrical index of hymn tunes based on a code indicating the number of syllables in each line of a hymn text. All hymn tunes that match this text with the correct number of syllables in each musical line are labeled with this same code. It is often also found at the top of the hymn right after the name of the tune.

As an illustration, consider the hymn tune "Beecher," which is often used with the text "Love Divine, All Loves Excelling." The meter for this tune is listed as 8.7.8.7.D. This means that there are eight syllables in the first line of the music, seven in the second, eight in the third, and seven in the fourth. The "D" stands for double, which means to repeat the meter of the first four lines. Here is the text of the first stanza of "Love Divine, All Loves Excelling" with the syllables numbered:

```
1     2 3     4 5     6 7 8
Love di-vine, all loves ex-cel-ling
```

```
1   2 3       4 5   6    7
Joy of heav'n, to earth come down,
```

```
1  2  3  4   5   6   7    8
Fix in us thy hum-ble dwell-ing,
```

```
1  2   3    4 5   6   7
All thy faith-ful mer-cies crown;
```

```
1 2   3    4  5 6   7   8
Je-sus, thou art all com-pas-sion;
```

```
1     2 3      4 5   6   7
Pure, un-bound-ed love thou art;
```

```
1  2 3 4    5   6 7 8
Vis-it us with thy sal-va-tion,
```

```
1   2   3 4   5    6    7
En-ter ev-ery trem-bling heart.
```

Since the text has a meter of 8.7.8.7.D., any other tune with that same code could be used with those words.

You will notice that the meters of many hymns are indicated by letters such as S.M., C.M., and L.M. rather than with numbers. S.M. (short meter) is the shorthand way of writing 6.6.8.6, the meter of a hymn such as "Blest Be the Tie That binds." C.M. (common meter) is 8.6.8.6., the meter of "O God Our Help in Ages Past." L.M. (long meter) is 8.8.8.8., the meter for "All People That on Earth Do Dwell."

Using the metrical index in your hymnal will enable you "mix and match" hymn tunes and texts, but you must always be sure that the mood fits and that the same syllables are stressed in the tune as in the words.

Other indexes frequently found in hymnals list authors, translators, or sources of words. You may not need this information very often, but when printing a worship service it is sometimes necessary to have some of this data for securing permission to reprint words or music.

Learning New Music

Learning sessions are a good way to introduce new or unfamiliar pieces. To try to use an unfamiliar piece would prove disruptive in a worship service, but a short period just before worship can be used to make the words and tune familiar.

Another way to stimulate the learning of new music is to avoid repeating the old familiar songs too often, taking care when planning a worship service not to use the first song that comes to mind. One way to help a group become acquainted with music is to use it as a prelude to the service.

The process of learning a new piece follows four steps:

1. Become familiar with the words, reading them aloud and discussing the meaning of any unfamiliar terms.
2. Listen to the tune, played by a skilled musician.
3. Sing the first stanza several times. Try to match the tempo to the music and the mood of the song.
4. Sing the whole piece through.

The Dramatic Arts and Worship

Think of a familiar parable of Jesus' and jot down the characters and an outline of the plot. In just ten minutes, brainstorm as many ways as possible to dramatize that parable. Then look back over your list and try to remember when you yourself have experienced a similar act of drama within worship.

From very early times, drama has been one of the elements of worship and celebration. In the Jewish Temple, the rituals of the various sacrifices held the worshipers in awe; Isaiah's conversion experience (Isaiah 6:1–8) was lofty pageantry; David and Miriam each in his or her own time danced to worship God. The Christian faith itself is often referred to as a divine drama of redemption.

Even today, we can look on the whole service of worship as a kind of drama with God as the audience. There are parts for the leader and congregation to play; there is a sense of movement from beginning to end; and there are one or more climaxes. Actions are used by a congregation to add a sense of dramatic impact to the words. Groups process and recess; people stand for singing, pass the peace, and move around for the offering even in a fairly simple service. Other congregational actions such as clapping, holding hands, walking forward for baptism or communion, and kneeling for prayers also increase the sense of worship as high drama.

For years Protestants relegated intentional dramatic presentations to special occasions, such as Christmas and Easter, but an increased interest in the arts has meant a broader use of specific dramatic forms. The dramatic arts, though, should be used in worship services carefully and in keeping with the integrity of worship. A congregation should never be left with the feeling that they have merely witnessed a drama preceded and followed by unrelated worship elements. Those who participate in a dramatic effort must do so in a spirit of worship.

Several types of dramatic materials that are easy to perform and can be made a part of a worship service without too much advance preparations are found in Part Two of this book. Other sources of materials are listed in the bibliography.

This chapter will deal with such forms as choral reading, plays, scenes, pageants, clowning and mime, dance, and storytelling.

Choral Reading

As discussed in the chapter "Using the Bible in Worship," choral reading can be done by the whole congregation if the material is available in their books or bulletins. In addition to the Bible, poetry, litanies, and special readings can be used. But there are times when a specific piece ought to be read by a group that has rehearsed in advance.

A speech choir gets its interpretive effects through the quality and timbre of the voices of its members. Usually the group is divided into sections, those with high or light voices in one group, those with low or heavy voices in another, with a group of medium voices carrying the bulk of the narration. A leader who has some skill and training is required for advanced or complicated choral speech, but a simple piece can be done effectively under the direction of a sensitive but untrained leader. A group can work with the leader to understand the meaning of the material; to perfect the arrangement of the voice parts (deciding on when heavy and light voices come in and which parts can be solos, duets, or trios); and to decide on dramatic effects. Sufficient rehearsal time must be allowed to ensure that the timing is well done and the speakers are clearly understood.

Many young people have had some introduction to choral reading at church, and a few will certainly be able to guide a beginning group. A singing choir might attempt some reading with the help of the choir director.

Plays and Musicals

A one-act play, well-rehearsed and costumed, may be the main part of a worship service. *The Terrible Meek* by Charles Rann Kennedy, for example, calls for only three characters and can be performed in the chancel with very simple costuming and uncomplicated lighting. The value of such a short drama is that there is no need for the interruption of intermissions or costume changes.

Whole dramas performed in a worship setting may become worship experiences in themselves, though greater skill is demanded of the performers to deal with more complex material. In looking for a play for so ambitious a project, remember that merely because a play has a religious subject it does not follow that it will be a good play or that it is appropriate in a worship setting. The play must be one that has the power to give an audience a true sense of communion with God, although it may not have an overt religious theme. Some examples are *Death of a Salesman* by Arthur Miller, *Diary of Anne Frank* by Frances Goodrich and Albert Hackett, *Murder in the Cathedral* by T. S. Eliot; *Androcles and the Lion* by George Bernard Shaw, and *The Flowering Peach* by Clifford Odets.

Occasionally the dialogue from a portion of a play may be used as a meditation for a worship service, spoken by two or three persons. This can be simpler than doing a whole play either acted out or just read with little or no costuming or stage setting.

Some possibilities are the trial scenes from either *Saint Joan* by George Bernard Shaw or *Joan of Lorraine* by Maxwell Anderson; Simeon's meditation and Herod's speech from W. H. Auden's *For the Time Being*; parts of *Murder in the Cathedral* by T. S. Eliot, *Gideon* by Paddy Chayefsky, and *J.B.* by Archibald MacLeish.

Musicals are another popular dramatic form for young people. *Jesus Christ, Superstar* by Andrew Lloyd Webber and Tim Rice, *Godspell* by John-Michael Tebelak and Stephen Schwartz, and *Joseph and the Amazing Technicolor Dreamcoat* by Andrew Lloyd Webber and Tim Rice are among the best known. Shorter musicals such as *Love, You Spoke a Word* by Ken Medema and *Moses and the Freedom Fanatics* by Hal H. Hopson are also usable in worship settings.

Pageants

To dramatize the sweep of religious history or to focus the emotions of a group on a contemporary religious or social problem, a pageant is often the best medium to use. A pageant utilizes many forms of dramatic arts such as music, choric speech, dance, drama, and pantomime and requires a large cast and narrator to carry the thread of the story. Although it demands a great deal of preparation and cooperation, it is a way to provide parts for a large number of people at a large gathering.

Clowning and Miming

Clowning is becoming popular for both young people and adults in churches across the country. There have been many good as well as bad experiences using clowns in worship services. Clowns can be a helpful way of bringing a new approach to familiar materials, and they can raise the consciousness of worshipers through exaggeration and humor. When their performance is poor, clowns prevent worship.

Perhaps the most meaningful statement about clowns in worship comes from Floyd Shaffer in the August 1981 issue of *Modern Liturgy*.[1]

> Clowns are not performers. Their clowning is a means through which tasks are accomplished. Clowning is a delivery system. The primary role of the clown is *to create an environment for the circus to happen.* In worship, leaders ought to be aware that the task is not to perform worship, but create an environment in which the people of God may worship. This is vital whether we are in the makeup or out of the makeup. When we as clowns reduce our worship to nothing but several well rehearsed skits, we slide into the performer role, and although we may look like clowns, clowning is not happening.

Miming is often categorized with clowning, although mimes are not necessarily clowns, and it is perfectly possible for clowns to speak as well as to remain silent. Mime is really just using nonverbal means entirely to convey a message. Miming can be done with a background of music as well as silence. Sometimes a reading is done in advance or even while a mime is performing. An extremely simple costume, whiteface, and few or no props are all that is needed.

Dance

There was a time when the idea of using dance in the church brought shocked faces and a sense of horror. But times have changed and a good performance by a dance group is appreciated in most congregations. A rhythmic choir (as it is sometimes called) "creates symbolic rhythmic movements and designs to interpret religious ideas and moods," says Margaret Palmer Fisk, author of the book *The Art of the Rhythmic Choir*[2] and one of the best-known people concerned with using dance in the church. Here again a good director and a finished performance are essential for a meaningful worship experience.

Storytelling

Storytelling is another form of dramatic arts that is useful in worship services. Stories can be passages of the Bible retold as narrative as well as tales drawn from our own personal experiences. Folk tales and biographies are good sources of information along with collections of stories of saints.

When preparing to tell a story, it is a good idea to learn as much as possible about the background and setting of the characters so that you can begin to feel what they felt. Some people find it helpful to picture each scene in their heads as if it were a film and then describe what is going on as they tell the story. It is also helpful to think through what can be seen, heard, touched, tasted, and smelled in each part of the story and include those sensory details in the retelling.

Most good storytellers do not memorize their stories but just learn the outline and then memorize words and phrases that are especially beautiful. It is also important to practice your story, especially in front of another person, before you use it in worship.

When it comes time to tell the story, try to relax and be yourself. Speak slowly and clearly and look directly at the congregation; when you are finished, just stop. A good story carries itself and does not need the storyteller to moralize or point out the meaning.

Visual Arts and Audiovisuals in Worship

Some people are visually oriented and others are hearing oriented. Still others are kinesthetically oriented, or mostly responsive to action and touch. Can you figure out which you are? Whether or not you are visually oriented, try for a moment to imagine how worship would differ for you if you could not see anything that was going on.

The use of visual art in the forms of stained glass, fabrics, paintings, and sculpture to lend dignity, atmosphere, and a focus for worship is a practice of long standing. Much of the art that fills museums today was originally created to decorate churches and cathedrals, frequently as a part of an elaborate altar. After centuries during which art was virtually banned from Protestant churches for fear that it would stimulate image worship, it is winning its way back into sanctuaries and classrooms.

Ways of Using Pictures

Focus of Attention

Church school classes and youth groups have found that a dignified and artistic center of attention helps create a worshipful atmosphere. In choosing pictures for this purpose, don't choose cheap illustrations just because the subject is religious. Good art deepens perceptions and leads to new ideas and religious feelings. Ideas can be evoked through what some call secular subjects or even through abstract forms. For biblical scenes, it is often wise to use a variety of pictures so that everyone remembers that a picture is an artist's concept of an event rather than a true record.

Theme for Meditation

Art may also be used as a theme or parable on which a worship meditation is based. This requires a careful study of a picture, just as a meditation based on a biblical passage requires a careful study of the Bible.

A picture that is to be used as the basis for a meditation must be large enough and clear enough to enable everyone in the room to see it during the service. It should be well lighted, possibly with a tensor or gooseneck lamp or spotlight arranged so that it will not throw glare into the eyes of the worshipers or onto the surface of the picture.

If the picture you want to use is not available in your church, public library, or resource center, or if you cannot purchase a print large enough to enable the entire group to see it from any point in the room, consider the possibility of obtaining a slide. It can then be projected on a screen placed behind your worship center or altar for the entire service.

When neither a large print nor a slide is available, don't overlook the possibility of obtaining a postcard reproduction or a reproduction from a magazine to show with an opaque projector on a screen. Occasionally postcards of famous paintings are available at a small enough cost so that each person may be given a copy to take home.

A number of meditations on well-known religious paintings put into a framework of worship are presented in the resource section. One way to deal with such a meditation is through probing questions to help a worshiper discover the meaning of the work. These questions would need to be worked out carefully in advance by the leader so that the conversation flows well. Another possibility is to let the worship leader prepare his or her own thoughts about the picture. Helpful material for such interpretations may be found in a number of books, although the most comprehensive is *The Gospel in Art* by Albert Edward Bailey.[3] This book is out of print but may be found in libraries.

Still another fruitful way of using pictures in worship is through comparison. Since many different artists have painted interpretations of Christ, you may find it interesting and worthwhile to make a comparison of a picture such as *Christ Mocked by Soldiers* by Georges Rouault with interpretations by artists of earlier centuries.

Original Materials

There should also be opportunities for artists within your congregation and even within the youth of the church to contribute to worship. Check around to see if any appropriate pieces are available. In addition, the production of banners, processional symbols, and other visual resources can allow everyone to contribute to the arts used in worship.

Ways of Using Audiovisuals

Slides, films, and filmstrips can enhance worship by focusing attention, creating an atmosphere, clearing the mind, stirring the emotions, and lifting the spirit. But more than usual care must be taken in planning and conducting any service of worship that includes audiovisual materials so that such mechanical details as lighting, timing, volume, and focus do not get in the way.

When using audiovisuals in a worship service, it is helpful to have the lights controlled by a rheostat so that they may be dimmed or raised gradually with no abrupt changes. When this is not possible, it may be desirable to keep the room lighting subdued after the showing and until the entire service has concluded and the worshipers have left the room. Beginning to put on some of the lights during the very last part of the film, filmstrip, or slide presentation also keeps the change in light level gradual and is preferable to an abrupt switch from dark to light.

A stark white screen standing at the front of a room, even when it is against a wall, is a distracting influence in a worship service. It is better to put it in place at the last minute or to have a slide already projected on the screen when the worshipers enter the room.

Check the room in advance to be sure there is an electrical outlet in a convenient place and that it is still live when the room lights are turned off. It is important to practice so that your timing is as good as possible. Sometimes recording the script before the showing makes the timing easier; other times, the immediacy of having a reader is more desirable.

Slides and Filmstrips

A single projected slide of a work of art, as was said above, can often prove more satisfactory than a print. In addition, single projected slides of other subjects can be used to set a mood and provide a focus for the entire service.

A series of slides can be used while a reading or music is presented or, sometimes for impact, in complete silence. Poetry and biblical readings lend themselves well to slides, but prayers and hymns may also be so illustrated. If a hymn is used for the framework, be sure it is a familiar one so that people can concentrate on the slides instead of having their eyes glued to the words of the hymn. The late Virgil Foster, editor of the *International Journal of Religious Education*, put together a series of nature scenes to illustrate the hymn "God, Who Touchest Earth With Beauty." It is offered here as an example.

Hymn lines	*Slides*
1. God, who touchest earth with beauty, Make my heart anew;	(sunset over a lake)
With thy Spirit recreate me, Pure and strong and true.	(young people on hill overlooking water)
2. Like thy springs and running waters Make me crystal pure;	(stream rushing over rapids)
Like thy rocks of towering grandeur Make me strong and sure.	(tall rocky mountain)
3. Like thy dancing waves in sunlight Make me glad and free;	(sun on lake)
Like the straightness of the pine trees Let me upright be.	(clump of tall trees)
4. Like the arching of the heavens Lift my thoughts above;	(clouded sky in distance)
Turn my dreams to noble actions— Ministries of love.	(view of Mt. Rushmore)
5. God, who touchest earth with beauty, Make my heart anew;	(trees with autumn coloring)
Keep me ever, by thy Spirit, Pure and strong and true. Amen.	(a young person)

Someone in your group or in the church may have a collection of slides that could be borrowed and arranged for use in worship. If not, try a local resource center or ask someone with a camera to begin taking the shots you need. "Write on" slides are another possibility, particularly if fairly abstract pictures are produced.

In choosing slides, keep in mind the possibility of contrasting scenes such as wealth and poverty, war and peace, hunger and plenty. The use of two slide projectors and screens adds to the possibilities.

A large number of filmstrips have been produced for educational purposes and some of them are also usable in worship. Look for those with an emotional impact rather than those with a story line.

Films and Videotapes

A short movie or part of one will often serve as an excellent meditation for worship, since films tend to have greater impact than still shots. If the film is especially emotional, it will be important to place it in a framework in the service and allow the participants to move carefully from the film to the next part of the service. Sometimes a moment of silence is needed to make the transition.

Videotapes are becoming popular in churches, but unless the equipment is available to provide a large image, they are best kept for teaching or entertainment purposes.

Worship in the Out-of-Doors

Jesus often preached or prayed in the out-of-doors on a mountain or in a boat to people gathered on the shore. Look up Luke 5:1–3, which describes Jesus preaching from a boat. If you were to plan a worship service in that setting, what would be the barriers to good worship? What problems might you encounter? What would be helpful about the setting?

Most people welcome opportunities to worship God in the out-of-doors—in temples not made by hands. In northern climates, summertime affords the best opportunity for outdoor worship services, but spring, fall, and even winter can be used. An Easter dawn service or a harvest home festival are possibilities to consider. Other occasions include a church school picnic or church picnic, summer camp, youth conferences and retreats, and a joint service of young people from several churches.

While any time of day is appropriate for worship, outdoor services are most often held either in the early morning or in the evening at sunset. A service around a campfire is best after dark.

When planning a worship service out-of-doors, leaders must guard against adopting pagan worship forms that lead to meditating on the sunset rather than on the God revealed in the sunset. It is not nature that Christians worship but nature's God. Even so, the natural environment should help shape the service and can be included in the plans. It would be a mistake merely to take an indoor service outside and ignore the surroundings.

Choosing a Suitable Place

Look for a spot near enough to be reached easily. It should be far enough away from traffic, however, to avoid distractions. If you are to worship at a lake or river site where there are motorboats, consider posting a sign in letters large enough to be read from the water "Quiet Please! Worship in Progress," or ask for volunteers to act as lookouts to try to divert boats.

The worship area may be a beauty spot near a stream or a lake in the woods. If your group is larger than twenty or thirty persons, the use of a hillside or a natural amphitheater will enable everyone to hear and see better.

A wise precaution is to check the area you plan to use a day or two before the meeting at the same hour that you will be gathering for your service in order to make sure there will be no glare from the sun. Check the acoustics also and determine if amplification is needed. When choosing leaders for outdoor services, it is important to find people who can project their voices.

Consider seating arrangements, especially if the ground is likely to be damp. Sometimes all that is necessary is to ask people to bring old blankets to sit on. If benches and chairs are provided for only part of the group, arrange these at the rear so that they do not obstruct the view of anyone sitting on the ground. Seating the group as compactly as possible will make it easier for them to hear as well.

If the property does not belong to the church, be sure to ask permission ahead of time to use it for worship purposes. This is important especially in public parks, where there may be regulations prohibiting the use of a loudspeaker system or the erection of a cross or religious symbol. If there are no objections, the use of a rustic cross or altar may help focus your worship.

Be sure to think through plans in case of rain. Some services can be moved indoors. Others could be held right in the rain or postponed until another date.

Planning the Music

A musical instrument that is portable enough to use out-of-doors, such as a trumpet, French horn, xylophone, or accordion, can add greatly to a service. Some churches own a small portable pump or electronic organ for outdoor use. Stringed instruments such as electric or folk guitars are especially suitable.

Only familiar tunes should be planned for outdoor worship where there will be no instrument available for accompaniment. If you have someone to pitch unaccompanied music, you are fortunate; otherwise, consider the use of a pitch pipe for the first note.

Avoid choosing long, slow hymns, or else sing only one or two stanzas, since groups tend to sing more slowly outdoors, especially when unaccompanied. If for some reason an unfamiliar hymn must be used, let a choir composed of several members of the group who have rehearsed it beforehand lead the group.

With good planning, worship in the out-of-doors can be meaningful to your group.

Preparing Original Materials

When children are little, they tend to create a lot of original materials such as stories and even prayers. When they grow older they do less of this. Young people vary a lot in how much they work on producing original materials. Why do you think this happens? What would be ways of encouraging people to create original materials all during their lives?

Sometimes, no matter how hard you look or how complete your file of worship materials may be, the poem or prayer you want is simply nowhere to be found. Rather than introduce an inappropriate element into the service, you will need to write your own. Much personal satisfaction as well as the realization of a growing sense of communion with God awaits you as well if you take time to write your own prayers, litanies, meditations, or even hymns.

It will be important to set yourself high standards. To fall into ruts of sentimentalism and doggerel is all too easy. Trite expressions may find their way into your prayers; poems or hymns may suffer from over-simplification of rhythm; prayers may sound abrupt, incomplete, or disjointed. Try instead to work from a clear idea of what you want to convey, take plenty of time to write, and allow others to enter the creative process with you. Reread Chapter Three and the section on inclusive language.

Writing a Prayer

It may seem too obvious to mention, but prayer should be directed toward God. It is never appropriate to use a prayer as a kind of catalog of announcements aimed at telling God what an individual or group is doing or as an expression of an opinion or an attempt to teach the praying group what God is like.

Some of the elements that may be appropriately included in prayers are as follows:

Adoration and praise express love for God and sometimes include affirmations of faith in God or recognition of God's attributes.

"Great art thou and greatly to be praised."
"We worship you, we adore you, we praise you."
"We praise your holy name."

Penitence or confession asks God's forgiveness for individual or group sins.

"Have mercy upon me, O God, . . . Wash me thoroughly from my iniquity, and cleanse me from my sin! [Psalm 51:1–2]."
"We ask your forgiveness for . . ."

Thanksgiving expresses gratitude for God's blessings and may be quite specific.

"We thank you for . . ."
"Praise God from whom all blessings flow."

Petition asks God for guidance and help for individuals and the group.

"Teach us to act more boldly in doing your will."
"Grant us wisdom, grant us courage."

Intercession asks God's help or blessing on others.

"We remember before you, O God, those who are ill."
"We pray for your servant (name), who . . ."

No prayer needs to include all these elements, but you may want to include several of them for a well-rounded prayer. Alternatively, you may wish to include prayers in several places in the service, keeping each one separate in type.

It would be well to begin your prayer with some form of direct address such as "Creator God" and to end it with a word of praise or a petition such as "We ask it in the name of Jesus Christ." It is also customary to end a prayer with the word Amen, which is actually an exclamation meaning "So be it!" or "I agree."

Some people find it comfortable to use the word you in addressing God, but others prefer to use the traditional language. If you use the latter, be sure to use "thou" as the subject of the verb, "thee" as the object, and "thy or thine" as the possessive form. For example.

"Thou hast been our dwelling place in all generations."
"Unto Thee we bring our offerings."
"Thy will be done."
"Thine is the kingdom."

If you use the older forms, be sure to use verbs in traditional language also. Reading of prayers and hymns written in these forms will make you more at home with them.

In addition to prayers by the leader, you might want to include some for congregational participation. Individuals may be encouraged simply to speak their own prayers. Another form is the bidding prayer (see Part Two for an example) where the leader suggests what the group is to pray about and then allows time for silent or spoken response.

Writing a Litany

A litany may be described as a responsive prayer in which the leader reads a part and the group responds with an appropriate phrase. Since a litany is a prayer, it may include one or more of the elements of prayer already described. Some responses may be

"We praise you, our Creator."
"We worship Thee, we praise Thee, we magnify Thy holy name."
"God have mercy upon us."

Usually in a litany the same responsive phrase is repeated four or five times. Sometimes when the mood of the litany changes, another response is used once or twice, though this is not always true. Frequently a final summary prayer to be read in unison concludes a litany.

The following is an example of a litany for young people.

✳ A Litany of Confession

LEADER: O God, we confess that we have often blurred the atmosphere with our noisy lives, and have not heard your call.

GROUP: Forgive us, we pray.

LEADER: We are part of the sin of our age. Hating war but being angry with our neighbor. Hating poverty but spending foolishly on ourselves. Hating hunger and wasting food.

GROUP: Forgive us, we pray.

LEADER: Do not let us remain slaves to our past, but help us this day and in the future to make our lives conform more closely to your will.

ALL: Amen.

A litany is perhaps the easiest kind of prayer for a group to write together. The ideas of the entire group should first be listed, then a section written about each idea or a combination of ideas. An appropriate response should be chosen and perhaps a summary section written for the end.

Preparing a Meditation or Sermon

A meditation or sermon is the way we share with others what we think God is saying to us, often through a particular passage of scripture. To be effective, a meditation needs to be thought-provoking, challenging, or inspiring; it should not be thought of as a lecture. Not every group of comments nor every story we may come upon is suitable for this purpose. The following are suggestions of types of materials that may prove helpful in planning a meditation.

> A poem with comments by the worship leader or with a spoken or silent prayer.
> A brief story of the life of some great Christian either of the present day or the past.
> A folk story that parallels the Christian message.
> An interpretation of a picture. (See Chapter 9 "Visual Arts and Audiovisuals in Worship" for suggestions.)
> An interpretation of a hymn. (Several examples are in the resource section.)
> Some item from the current news with comments as to its meaning for Christian living.
> A short, inspiring story or paragraph from a book or a magazine with comments by the worship leader.
> A story from personal experience, with comments or without.
> A Bible passage and discussion of its message for the group. You will want to use the Bible dictionary and commentary to give you background for whatever you choose.

Meditations can take the form of a film or other audiovisual presentation as well as a dramatic form. It is well to vary the form and to use the pattern that best carries out the theme of the service.

Writing a Hymn

With today's concern for the use of more-inclusive language and the need to write hymns focusing on peace and justice, there has been an upsurge in the writing of new hymns. Although hymns are probably the most difficult form of worship materials to create, if someone in your group has a way with words, he or she might be encouraged to write a hymn. If rhyme is too difficult, try using blank verse that fits a standard hymn meter or familiar popular or folk tune.

A good way to begin is to write additional verses to some familiar hymn such as "Our God, Our Help in Ages Past" or "Go, Tell It on the Mountain." Hymns with phrases that repeat such as "When Morning Gilds the Skies" are especially easy to work with.

Here are some suggestions for beginners:

Choose a theme or phrase that is appealing and well worded.
Make a list of ideas that might be included in your hymn. Add appropriate rhyming words if they occur to you.
Adopt a hymn tune that is familiar and has an obvious rhythm.
Write as much of the hymn as you can, forgetting about rhyme and leaving out lines entirely in places where they do not come to you easily.
Go back to those lines that need working on, rephrasing others as you go along.
Sing the hymn several times aloud to polish the rough edges.
Put it away and come back to it later to rework any parts that now seem to be inappropriate or trite.
Let someone else sing it with you and make comments to help your work.
Finally, share your hymn with your group.

Locating Resources for Worship

When you need to choose a hymn for a worship service, how do you go about it? Where do you look for ideas for prayers or meditations?

A wealth of resources is available for any youth group to use to enrich its services of worship. There are prayers, poems, and hymns that have been handed down from generation to generation throughout the long and colorful history of the church. There are poems, prayers, hymns, and other materials being written today and available in books, magazines, and pamphlets.

If you have familiarized yourself with this book, you have already entered the front room of a vast storehouse of printed worship materials. But occasions will arise when your needs are not met by this book, and you will want to look for or write new materials. Here are some clues for your search.

Hymnals

In addition to containing hymns, most hymnals have a section devoted to worship materials, including prayers, responsive readings, calls to worship, benedictions, litanies, and sometimes poems and short meditations. The hymns themselves will frequently be useful as prayers and meditations when read without the music. "We Praise Thee, O God" can be used as a prayer and "Every Star Shall Sing a Carol" can be read without the refrain as a poem-meditation. When in doubt about using words of a hymn, read them aloud to yourself before making your choice.

The Book of Worship

Become familiar with the book of worship used in your own denomination. Though it contains forms for conducting the sacraments, funerals, and weddings, which only a minister would use, it also usually includes a treasury of prayers and responsive readings as well as a listing of Bible passages for each Sunday as well as festivals of the church year.

The book will probably draw heavily on your denominational heritage of worship resources and for that reason will be of special interest to your group. Your pastor will be glad to let you look at a copy so you may decide whether to buy one for the group's use.

Periodicals and Curriculum

Some religious magazines such as denominational periodicals or Christian education publications contain very usable worship materials that are worth saving for future reference. Poems and meditations as well as prayers appear in devotional booklets such as *These Days* and *The Upper Room*. Be sure, though, to examine these materials thoroughly to be sure they are appropriate for group worship, since they were originally planned for private devotional use.

Church school curriculum materials often contain worship resources and suggestions. Check to see if you can search through out-of-date materials before they are thrown out. If you see anything useful in current materials, make a note of its location for future reference.

Your Church or Pastor's Library

Most ministers are glad to help interested and responsible young people learn how to use the books in their personal libraries. They often own collections of prayers and books of worship from other denominations, as well as books for personal devotions and collections of sermons.

Even a small church can maintain a church library. If your church does not have one, perhaps this book plus several others of worship resources can become the core of a church reference library or a youth worship shelf. Visit the libraries of other churches in your area also. Churches are often delighted to see young people interested in worship and are willing to loan books to other churches.

Nonchurch Sources

Poetry and prose selections appropriate for use in worship services may frequently be found in high school literature texts as well as in general books, both fiction and nonfiction. Similarly, daily and Sunday newspapers and general magazines often contain materials that can be adapted for use in meditations or that spark an idea. Once you begin planning a worship service, you can keep the theme in mind in your daily life and be alert for whatever appears.

Keeping Track of Resources

There is no single best way to keep a file of worship resources, but your rule should be "the simpler, the better." The main thing is to be able to locate what you want when you want it.

One easy method is a group of eight to ten file folders. Some of the following categories would be useful:

calls to worship	poems
special hymns	meditations
prayers and litanies	benedictions
responsive readings	complete worship services
offertory sentences and prayers	

If you find materials in a book that you cannot clip from or copy, put a file card in the folder with a description of the material and its location.

Whenever you clip or copy material, be sure to make a note of where you found it and the author's name. If you are able to find out where and when it was first printed, it is important to note that information also.

Be careful to honor the copyright when you reproduce material for the use of groups. Normally you can obtain permission to reproduce material unless you intend to sell the book or booklet. It may seem like an unnecessary burden to write for permission, especially in these days when copying machines are available in so many places. The original author, however, as well as the publisher, has an investment to protect; it is, in effect, stealing to use reprinted material without permission. The copyright also helps to assure that the text is accurate.

Once you begin gathering resources for worship you will see materials everywhere. It can be a real adventure.

Organizing to Plan for Worship

Read or reread the three vignettes at the beginning of Chapter 1. Which of these most resemble what goes on in your group? What do you think the first steps should be to become better organized? Read this chapter and then talk or think about it again.

Any group accustomed to worshiping together regularly or whose members are themselves responsible for planning and leading worship for others soon feels the need for a small committee on worship. This committee can be given the responsibility of coordinating the planning and preparation of worship activities, securing and training the leaders, and maintaining the standards set up by the larger group.

Groups differ and the composition of the committee as well as its duties will be governed by the type of organization and the frequency of worship planning. The worship committee for a church school class will be relatively small and informal. A large, active youth group may need a six- to-ten-person committee, while a small group might just need two or three persons. A small Bible study group may designate one of its members for a short period of time and then rotate the responsibility to others in the group.

It is advisable either to ask for volunteers or to appoint people who have some natural inclination for, or previous experience in, planning worship services. Enthusiasm for creating worship services can awaken appreciation and interest others. Persons willing to serve on a worship committee are usually not hard to find if they know that the actual responsibility for leading worship is to be shared by the members of the group.

The Job of a Worship Committee

Following are suggestions of ways in which a worship committee might work to help involve other young people in finding meaning in worship services.

Planning Ahead

If there is a regular weekly, semimonthly, or monthly worship service to plan, the worship committee would do well to project its plans from three to six months ahead. If worship services are to be directly related to discussions scheduled by the group, the themes of the discussions will inform the type of worship the committee will plan. If the worship committee is planning for a church school class or department, the members will need to check with the teachers for help in determining the direction the curriculum will take.

If the group is only planning for special services or special events, long-range planning will allow for greater creativity with the service. The first meeting could determine the theme and some basic possibilities. Members of the group would then have opportunity to dream up ideas and research materials before the group meets again to further their planning. A third meeting to finalize the service and perhaps a fourth to rehearse with everyone involved should be allowed for in the schedule.

The very small group often meets with several obstacles in planning an extensive program. It is probably better to plan fewer services and do them well than to try to do too much. It is important in a small group especially to rotate responsibilities instead of depending on the same person for the same jobs all the time. Worship in a small-group setting can be enhanced by asking a special adult to work with the group occasionally or by joining with other churches nearby for special occasions.

Assigning Leaders

When there are a number of services to plan and lead, individual members of the group should be asked to accept responsibility for specific services. When such assignments are made well in advance, most group members will see the fairness of everyone agreeing to take a turn. A master list giving the dates of services with the names of the leaders should be posted or distributed as a reminder. One member of the worship committee can act as coordinator to remind people of their responsibilities. Any needed trading of jobs on the part of those appointed can be reported to the coordinator.

If there is only one major service coming up, such as a Youth Sunday service, the worship committee itself may want to do the planning. When planning is complete, it will be important to involve other members in leading the service so as not to make the worship committee the only ones involved in worship.

Educating People About Worship

A major contribution that a worship committee might make to the group is to provide training in leading worship and in worship itself. The committee might decide to invite the pastor or a trained lay person to meet with the entire group to explain the meaning of worship and the forms it may take. Or, they might plan their own program of training drawing on chapters in this book.

If the group is a church school class with limited time and less flexibility in programming, the committee might plan to devote several worship periods to education instead of worship. A worship course is included in the User's Guide at the beginning of this book. There are also available several pieces of curriculum on worship for use by the church-school class. Don't overlook the possibilities of using curriculum designed for junior high students or adults in this field.

Establishing a Worship Library or File

The worship committee should regard it as one of their functions to see that a worship library or at least a file of resources is available to persons assigned to lead services. Suggestions for a resource file and books that might be in your worship library are a part of Chapter 12, "Locating Resources for Worship."

Evaluating

An important function of the worship committee is that of keeping worship services on a truly worshipful level. Special services should be evaluated by the planners and worship leaders within the week. Ongoing programs of worship can be evaluated every two or three months. As a framework for evaluation, ask such questions as the following:

What helped people worship?
What got in the way of worship?
How could we improve?

The last question might lead the group toward some kinds of specific actions that would improve worship the "next time." Keep a simple record of the evaluation along with a copy of the service in your worship file so that future committees and planners might learn from your mistakes.

The Job of an Adult Adviser

The adult adviser can be of help to the worship committee in many ways. If the committee has responsibility for worship in a church school, one of the teachers may be the adviser. Otherwise, the youth-group adviser or pastor may need to work with the young people in planning worship.

Some of the ways an adult adviser may help include the following:

Act as a resource person when the committee is meeting to draft long-range plans.

Coach the committee members and worship leaders as they actually plan.

Take part in worship occasionally to model ways of leading worship or new forms of worship.

Help the committee to discover available resources in the church and community.

Represent the worship needs and interests of youth in meetings of adult committees and board of the church.

Worship along with the young people.

PART TWO

Resources for Worship

Part Two is a treasury of resources. Each chapter contains a few complete services plus additional material such as poems, prayers, readings, scripture suggestions, recommended hymns, and "idea starters" to stimulate the creative process. The selection of materials is meant to spark creativity rather than to be a group of predigested, "canned" worship services. Only a few services have been completely worked out to give users a feeling for combining appropriate materials into a whole. The resources are drawn from a variety of traditions and include some original material. They use inclusive language where possible.

Resources for Special Days and Seasons

Advent, Christmas, and New Year

The custom of lighting Advent candles has become popular in many churches. If a group meets several times during Advent, they may want to use Advent candles in their worship. The appropriate service might also be used for any single occasion along the way.

In medieval times, when this observance seems to have originated, rings of candles were hung from the ceilings of churches or arranged on the mantelshelf of Christian homes. In Germany, in particular, a wreath of evergreens with four candles, known as an Advent wreath, was set up in every household. The evergreen is a symbol of life; the circle stands for eternity; and the lighting of the candles symbolizes the coming of light into the world with Jesus.

Arrange four candles around a large candle in the center, called the Christ candle. Evergreens can be added to make a wreath. One of the small candles is lit each week during the service. The center candle should be lit before worshipers arrive, as, on the second, third, and fourth Sundays, are the candles lit on the previous Sundays.

First Sunday in Advent: A Suggested Service

✳ Call to Worship

> Prepare the way of the Lord,
>   make straight in the desert a highway for our God.
> And the glory of the Lord shall be revealed
>   and all flesh shall see it together (Isa. 40:1–11).

✳ Hymn

"Watchman, Tell Us of the Night"

✳ Scripture Reading

A Prophecy of Christ's Coming — Isa. 40:1–11

✳ Lighting of the First Advent Candle
(The leader should explain briefly the custom of lighting Advent candles.)

✳ Prayer

We cry out, O God, impatient for your kingdom.
    We want the roughness in our own lives to be polished,
    and our all-too-human instinct toward violence to be
        banished.
But you, O God, accept us as we are.
    You comfort us with your forgiveness.
    In the Christ who is coming into our lives, You care for us as a
        shepherd cares for the youngest lambs.
So, during these days of Advent, O God, we are grateful for
        your signs of promise:
    We look beyond the Star in the night to the morning of
        Christ's birth in each of us. Amen.

— J.M.B.

✳ Hymn

"O Come, O Come, Emmanuel"

✳ Benediction

Arise, shine, for your light has come,
    and the glory of the Lord has risen upon you.
And the nations shall come to your light,
    and kings to the brightness of your rising (Isa. 60:1,3).

Second Sunday in Advent: A Suggested Service

✳ **Call to Worship**

> Sing for joy, O heavens, and exult,
>   O earth;
> break forth, O mountains, into singing!
> For the Lord has comforted the people,
> and will have compassion on the afflicted (Isa. 49:13).

✳ **Hymn**

> "Come, Thou Long-expected Jesus"

✳ **Scripture Readings**

> Old Testament prophecy — Isaiah 61:1–3
> New Testament fulfillment — Luke 4:16–24, 28–30

✳ **Lighting of the Second Advent Candle**
(Remember, the first candle and the Christ candle need to be lit before the worship service begins. The leader can repeat the explanation of the lighting of the Advent candles and/or the relation of the Old Testament prophecy to the New Testament fulfillment.)

✳ **Hymn**

> "Hail to the Lord's Anointed"

✳ **Prayer**

> Come into our lives, Christ Jesus!
>   Come with the good tidings of joy,
>   for though we enjoy many comforts
>   we are often afflicted by the poverty of our faith:
>   we need your guiding Spirit.
> Come and proclaim liberty to us, as to the slaves.
>   Open the doors of prejudice and hatred that imprison
>   each of us.

Come and heal our broken hearts — for with sad
    despair we see how we are held captive by
    selfishness and by war.
Come into our lives this Advent, setting us free
    to sing your praises and to be heralds of your peace.
    Amen.

                                        — J.M.B.

✳ Benediction

the same as the first week

Third Sunday in Advent: A Suggested Service

✳ Call to Worship

Sing and rejoice, O daughter of Zion;
    for lo, I come and I will dwell in the midst of you,
    says the Lord (Zech. 2:10).

✳ Hymn

"What Child Is This?"

✳ Scripture Readings

Old Testament prophecy — Isaiah 11:1–4
New Testament fulfillment — Matthew 2:1–9

✳ Lighting of the Third Advent Candle
(Use one of the meditations in the following section or one you have made up.)

✳ Hymn

"As With Gladness Those of Old"

✳ Prayer

> O God, our Advent journey is like the travels
>   of those Three Pilgrims who followed your Star.
> They were wise enough to seek wisdom and understanding.
>   With all their wealth, they sought the Spirit of Counsel and
>   Might.
>   They represented the world's power — yet they yearned for
>   righteousness and equity.
> So let your Spirit rest upon us:
>   Bring us wisdom and understanding.
>   In the Baby of Bethlehem, we seek a demonstration of your
>   faithful judgment upon us and upon all your people. Amen.
> — J.M.B.

✳ Benediction

the same as the first week

Fourth Sunday in Advent: A Suggested Service

✳ Call to Worship

> Joy to the world! the Lord in come;
> Let earth receive her king.

✳ Hymn

"Joy to the World"

✳ Scripture Readings

Old Testament prophecy — Isaiah 9:2–7
New Testament fulfillment — Luke 2:1–14

✳ Lighting of the Fourth Advent Candle
(A Christmas poem or a meditation would be appropriate here.)

✳ Hymn

any Christmas hymn

✳ Prayer

Dear God:
We come to Bethlehem to see the mystery.
   We think of ourselves as enlightened people.
   But in a strange way, we walk in darkness.
   As we approach Christmas we see, by contrast, a great Light.
And—though we have had every reason to be happy — we now
   know a greater joy.
Though it is hard to comprehend,
   we see that the Child that is born in each of us
   is a Wonderful Counselor and the Prince of Peace.
We sing for joy as we discover that there is no end to his peace.
And so we shout: Let earth receive the King! Amen.

                                         — J.M.B.

✳ Benediction

as before

Resources for Christmas Eve or Christmas Day

✳ Call to Worship

LEADER: It was cold, and Mary and Joseph were fearful.

GROUP: But that did not stop the birth.

LEADER: They were poor and had no room waiting for them.

GROUP: But that did not stop the birth.

LEADER: They were uncertain what God wanted from them.

GROUP: But that did not stop the birth.

LEADER: And today we are still sometimes cold and fearful, certainly
poor in so many ways and without the rooms we need, and
unclear about what God wants of us.

GROUP: But that did not stop the birth. Be born in us today. Amen.[1]

✴ A "Lined-out" Invocation
(The leader says a line and the congregation repeats it.)

God of Mary and Joseph,
God of the shepherds,
God of the Wise Men,
Our God;

God of the manger,
God of the cross,
God of the Church,
Our God;

God of Bethlehem,
God of Jerusalem,
God of _____ (your town)
Our God;

Give us, we pray, faith;
Give us, we pray, hope;
Give us, we pray, love;
Give us, we pray, joy;

That the Spirit of Christ will be born in us;
That Christ's way will be our way;
Christ's promises, our promises;

In Christ's blessed name we pray,
Amen.

— James O. Gilliom[2]

✴ The Decisive Babies of the World
Reading

We often learn in school about the decisive battles of history. But now Christmas comes again, engaging the thought and warming the heart of multitudes around the globe, and it concerns not a decisive battle but a decisive baby. "Unto us a child is born, unto us a son is given."

Even today, when all the world is obsessed with the fear and clash of arms, Christmas suggests how much more decisive a baby can be than a battle. When Jesus was born in Bethlehem, what were the decisive elements in the world's life? Surely, with Tiberius upon his throne, the Roman Empire's vast extent and power, and Caesar's legions trampling every road — any realistic mind would have pointed to such potent factors as the determining factors of the day.

As for a baby, born of a lowly mother in obscure Bethlehem upon the far fringes of the Empire, it would have been madness then to have supposed that almost two thousand years later millions of us would be singing of that event,

> Yet in thy dark street shineth
> The everlasting light;
> The hopes and fears of all the years
> Are met in thee tonight.

That is the miracle of Christmas — that a baby can be so decisive.
— **Harry Emerson Fosdick**[3]

✳ Enrollment in Bethlehem
Reading

In 1566 Pieter Brueghel the Elder painted a picture called *Enrollment in Bethelem*. The setting is not Oriental or Arabic or Palestinian. It is a sixteenth-century European village, probably much like ones Brueghel himself had known and lived in. The hard-packed ground is covered with snow, and on the frozen river two small boys are learning to skate. A woman is gathering firewood. Three men carrying heavy loads approach from one side. Around the two windows open for business at the front of what appears to be an inn, twenty or so people are clustered, trying to pay their taxes. Two men at the windows, perhaps a trifle hassled by the taxpayers, are carefully listing the enrollment in a large book. Just to one side of the gathered citizens, a man and two women are butchering a pig, winter being the correct time for such a project. On the other side of the picture, two children are whipping their tops; others are having a snowball fight. A woman is clucking over a wagon with a broken wheel. A man is coming out of a shabby hut.

Almost unnoticed, although in the center of the picture, a man leads a donkey on which a robed woman is seated. Neither has a halo. Nor is there a shaft of light from heaven spotlighting their entry into the town. The taxpayers and hog butchers and top spinners do not turn from their work to marvel at the arrival of the man and the woman.

And yet, in the midst of the ongoing life of the village, the greatest drama of the ages is about to take place.

Six hundred years before Caesar Augustus sent out his decree that all the world should be enrolled, farseeing Zephaniah wrote about the coming of the Son of God. "Be glad and rejoice with your whole heart. . . . The King of Israel, the Lord is in the midst of you, and you shall see disaster no more."

Ah, yes! In the midst of busy Bethlehem, in the midst of Brueghel's sixteenth-century retelling of it, and in the midst of our lives — Emmanuel! And we shall see disaster no more. For after the Christmas event, we are able to meet whatever life has to offer.

✳ Lest We Fail to See the Star

Eternal God, guard us, lest we fail to see the Star. We are too much taken up with our gifts, our cards, our parties. The world around us is taken over by the ring of the cash registers and hardly hears the ringing of the Christmas bells. Let Christmas come to us quietly and let us come to Christmas quietly, bearing as gifts our lives dedicated to Christ. Amen.

— J.M.B.

✳ The Work of Christmas
Poem

> When the song of the angel is stilled,
> When the star in the sky is gone,
> When the kings and princes are home,
> When the shepherds are back with their flock,
> The work of Christmas begins:
> to find the lost,
> to heal the broken,
> to feed the hungry,
> to release the prisoner,
> to rebuild the nations,
> to bring peace among people,
> to make music in the heart.

— Howard Thurman[4]

✳ Benediction

> May the God of the manger dwell always within you;
> The God of the shepherds, guide you to a new birth;
> And the God of the Magi give you the gift of eternal life. Amen.

— B.J.B.

✳ Idea Starters

If your group is planning a series of services during Advent, make a banner that changes or has something added to it each week and use this as your central visual piece.

Plan a service for your church's Advent workshop or the Hanging of the Greens ceremony.

Choose carols and scripture readings that go together to build a service by alternating music and the spoken word. For example, read Luke 2:8–15 and then sing "While Shepherds Watched Their Flocks by Night."

New Year's Eve or New Year's Day: A Suggested Service

The worship center could include a calender or star map or a map of space. For New Year's Eve, a clock should be in plain sight so that when the hour of midnight comes it can be seen by everyone.

✷ Call to Worship

The heavens are telling the glory of God and the firmament proclaims God's handiwork (Psalm 19:102).

✷ Hymn

"Praise to God, Immortal Praise"

✷ Scripture Reading

Psalm 121 or a recording of "He Watching Over Israel" from the oratorio *Elijah* by Mendelssohn. The following is an adaption of Leslie F. Brandt's version of Psalm 121:

> Where should I look for help in my need?
> To majestic mountain peaks that probe our skies
>   or to giants of industry that hem in our cities?
> To satellites that circle our world
>   or to computers that store up our knowledge?
>
> The answer to my problems
>   and the fulfillment of my needs
> must come from God
>   from God who created skies and mountains
>   and people to dwell in their midst.

God is a great God who knows our every desire,
   whose watchful eye is upon us night and day.
We can make no move without God's knowledge.
God's concern for God's children is constant;
   God's love for them is eternal.

And thus the Lord will keep you,
Shielding you from the forces of evil
   as a shade tree shields you
      from the rays of the blazing sun.

God does care for you,
   and God will fight with you
      against the enemies of your soul.
Whether you be coming or going,
   God knows the course you take,
     And God will go before you.

— **Leslie F. Brandt**[5]

✳ Group Discussion

Have the group as a whole or in small groups share with one another
the remembrances of the year past including happy, sad, and funny
things that happened. Then have each person share one hope for the
year to come.

✳ A Season for Everything
Reading
(For three readers and the congregation.)

LEADER: There's a season for everything under the sun,

  GROUP: A time to do and a time to be done,

LEADER: A time to laugh

  GROUP: And a time to cry,

LEADER: A time to live

  GROUP: And a time to die,

(Alternate readers 1 and 2.)

1: A time for dying and a time for rebirth.
2: A time for the spirit and a time for earth.
1: A time for laughter, a time for tears.
2: A time for courage and a time for fear.

1: A time to cling and a time to release.
2: A time for war and a time for peace.
1: A time to talk and a time to be still.
2: A time to care and a time to kill.
1: A time alone. A time for romance.
2: A time to mourn. A time to dance.
1: A time to keep. A time to lose.
2: A time to be told. A time to choose.
1: A time to tear down. A time to rebuild.
2: A time to be empty. A time to be filled.
1: A time to welcome and to send away.
2: A time to complain and a time to pray.
1: A time to share and a time to save.
2: A time to break rules. A time to behave.
1: A time to free and a time to bind.
2: A time to search and a time to find.
1: A time to plant and a time to uproot.
2: A time to be barren. A time to bear fruit.

1: A time of plenty.	2: A time of need.
1: A time to follow.	2: A time to lead.
1: A time to give.	2: A time to take.
1: A time to bend.	2: A time to break.
1: A time to hurt.	2: A time to heal.
1: A time for secrets.	2: A time to reveal.
1: A time to let go.	2: A time to hold.
1: A time to be young.	2: A time to grow old.
1: A time to rip open.	2: A time to mend.
1: A time to begin,	2: and a time to end.

LEADER: There's a season for everything under the sun,

GROUP: A time to do and a time to be done.

LEADER: A time to laugh

GROUP: And a time to cry,

LEADER: A time to live,

GROUP: And a time to die.[6]

✳ God the Beginning and the End
Prayer

O God, you are the beginning and the end; you set the stars in their places, and filled the earth with its fulness; we come to you in prayer. We see only our moment of time but you behold the end from the beginning. We know only our little circles of friends and acquaintances; but you number all humanity as your children. Teach us that you are still our guide and our comrade. Remind us that the vastness of the world has not pushed us out of your sight, nor the multitude of people blotted us out from your vision. Teach us that you are in our hearts and in our minds, closer to us than breathing, nearer than hands and feet. Teach us that as you are the God of history, so too you rule over every moment, including this one. We ask it in the name of Jesus Christ who began time anew and made us new creatures.

— **Allen Hackett**[7]

✳ Benediction

The steadfast love of God never ceases, God's mercies never come to an end. Amen (Lam. 3:22).

✳ Idea Starters

If the worship is in an appropriate setting, such as around a fireplace, have persons write down on paper unhappy experiences of the past year and as a group burn the pieces of paper.

As a symbol of the fresh year, give participants new spiral notebooks in which they can begin reflections on the year ahead.

Lent, Holy Week, and Easter

Early Lent

The nails of the cross would make a useful theme for the beginning of Lent. Square nails could be given to each person to carry during Lent as a daily reminder of his or her commitment to Christ. On Easter these nails could be placed in the offering as a symbol of renewal.

✳ The Nails of the Cross
Reading

During World War II the cathedral at Coventry, England, was largely destroyed by incendiary bombs dropped by German planes. The roof burned and collapsed, the interior furnishings burned, but the charred walls remained. During the cleanup of the ruins, a number of large nails were found among the charred timbers. They had been used in the construction of the roof and were thought by some to be reminiscent of the type used in the first century to nail victims to a cross for crucifixtion. A cross was formed with several of these large nails and placed on the charred altar of the cathedral ruins. A short time later, this cross was circulated among the various churches of the Coventry parish, remaining for a day or longer on the altar of each specific church. The spiritual impact was tremendous as the members of the various churches were reminded of their cathedral and also of the nails that held Christ to the cross.[8]

Maundy Thursday or Good Friday: A Suggested Service

✳ **Setting**
(Place one candle on the altar or worship table and six candles on stands, three on each side of the table. Readers should sit in the front row and come forward in pairs to stand by their candles. As each person finishes reading, he or she should put out the candle with a candle snuffer. When the pair finishes, they should both return to their seats.

Select music from your own hymnal that is appropriate for Good Friday. Possibilities are "I Wonder as I Wander," "O Sacred Head Now Wounded," "Jesus Walked This Lonesome Valley," and "Were You There." It is best if participants are seated throughout the whole service and then asked to leave silently at the end.)

✳ **Music for Meditation.**
This can be a record or tape.

✳ **Silence**

✳ **Scripture Readings**

> The prayer in Gethsemane — Mark 14:32–42
> The betrayal and arrest — Mark 14:43–52

✳ **Hymn**

✳ **Scripture Readings**

> Jesus before the Sanhedrin — Mark 14:53–65
> Peter's denial — Mark 14:66–72

* Hymn

* Scripture Readings

Jesus before Pilate — Mark 15:1–15
Jesus mocked, crowned with thorns, and crucified — Mark 15:16–27

* Hymn
(During this hymn the leader should put out the center candle.)

* Is It I, Lord?
Prayer

> Is it I, Lord?
> Is it I who denied you as Peter did?
> Is it I who betrayed you as Judas did?
> Am I one in the crowd who said, "Hosanna" one day,
>   and then a few days later cried, "Crucify"?
>
> Have I denied you those times when I have denied people their
>   rights?
> Denied people—even in my family—the right to think and be
>   themselves?
> Denied that there is injustice in the world
>   when it doesn't seem to affect me?
>
> Is it I, Lord, when I looked the other way
>   when someone was reaching out for help?
>   when I failed to stand up for friends in school,
>   when everyone seemed to be picking on them?
>   when I did not express my faith because it seemed unpopular?
>
> Is it I, Lord, who have yelled, "Crucify"
>   when my prayers were not answered as I thought they should
>   be?
> Is it I who have turned against you
>   when my faith conflicts with my social life or my politics?
> Am I one of the crowd who yelled, "Crucify"?
>
> Yes, Lord, it is I.
>   All of us have denied you in our own ways.
>   Each of us has betrayed you through our actions.
>   We are the crowd who turned against you.

O God, come to us in this time of darkness before the Easter
dawn.
Come to us and forgive us.
Strengthen us that we may grow in our faith—
and live that faith in every area of our lives.
Bind us together in the darkness as we pray together:
Our Father. . . .

— **Herbert Yeager**[9]

(The room lights should be raised slightly and people should be asked to leave in silence.)

✳ **Paradox**
Prayer

Father,
we have come to call this Friday "Good."
This day of whipping, stumbling, plotting,
nails and tears,
and determined mindless missing of the point.
This day on which your Son is hated to death.
This day on which your Word is pinned up against the sky
and silenced.
This day on which prophecies have their moment of truth,
and in the incredible desolation
of the after-noon Calvary
some are indeed heard to say,
"My God, he must have been the one. . . ."
We have come to call this Friday, "Good."
We come, Father, and ask once more the grace of retrospect
as we sit again at the feet
of this specific darkness

pain

absurdity

failure

lack of power

and last-breathing.

We ask to absorb the day's darknesses,
knowing them in our many selves.
We need to gently, but again,
sense ourselves and times
as whipper

stumbler

plotter

nailer and nailed.

We need to know the broken Lord
 in these our heres and nows.
We have come to call this Friday "Good."
And it is perhaps because
 it is salutary for us
 to know again . . . again . . .
   that your Son stood still for death
   because only in the utter completeness
     of that anguished handing over
   could the word *life*
   could the word *peace*
   could the words *whole* and *heal*
     be renamed in truth.
Which is to say redeemed.
Father, we have come to call this Friday "Good."
Absorb us in your silent sense of it.
Grace us with its goodness. Amen.

— **Loretta Whalen Force**[10]

✴ Idea Starters

Write a play from the story of the Last Supper using your imagination
concerning the characters of the group and what they did as they arrived
and as they left, and concerning the people in the kitchen.

An Easter Sunrise Service

✴ The Days of Holy Week

*(Sing a Palm Sunday hymn. Intersperse the remaining readings with hymns or
music sung by individuals or small groups. For the day of waiting try a quiet
instrumental piece and after the Easter Sunday reading sing "Christ the Lord Is
Risen Today." Close with a prayer.)*

Palm Sunday: The Day of Temporary Triumph — Mark 11:1–10
Monday: The day of emotion — Mark 11:15–18
Tuesday: The day of controversy — Matthew 21:14–16

Wednesday: The day of anointing — Mark 14:3–9
Thursday: The day of fellowship — Mark 14:17–26
Friday: The day of suffering — Mark 15:12–20
Saturday: The day of waiting
Easter Sunday: The day of resurrection — Luke 24:1–9

✴ I Feel It, I Know It
Poem
(To be spoken at the moment of sunrise.)

> I feel it, I know it, I am lit by the sun,
> The glow and the glory of life has begun;
> Within my soul blazes the enkindling flame
> On the altar upraised to the uttermost Name.
> I'm alight, I'm afire, with a radiance born
> Of the sunrise immortal, the ineffable dawn.
>
> I am one with the light of the stars in the sky,
> And one with the splendor that shines from on high;
> Time holds me no more, nor space hath dominion
> To limit the flight of my loftiest pinion;
> I am free as the air, and swift as the light
> Of the glimmering flashes that break in the night.
>
> I prophesy sunrise — lo, the time is at hand
> When glory shall break on this war-weary land,
> And dark doubts shall be gone, and clear faith shall renew
> The face of the earth with the radiant dew
> Of the morning immortal, and the fragrance of heaven
> Breathe forth from a million new hearts vision-given.
>
> I prophesy sunrise — for I feel it, I know
> By the thrill in my soul, by the quivering glow
> Of the light in my life that is bursting anew
> With the dreams that are real and the faith that is true,
> As sure as I live is the truth, glory-shod —
> I am lit by the sun — I am one with my God.
>
> — **Oliver Huckel**[11]

✴ The Adoration of the Risen Lord
(The congregation, led by a choir or song leader, should sing the alleluias. Try the melody from "The Strife Is O'er" using the final alleluia until the last phrase and ending with the triple alleluia from the beginning.)

LEADER: Now upon the first day of the week, very early in the morning, the women came unto the sepulchre, bringing the spices which they had prepared. And they found the stone rolled away from the sepulchre.

CONGREGATION: Alleluia!

LEADER: And the women departed quickly from the sepulchre with fear and great joy. And Jesus met them saying, All hail.

CONGREGATION: Alleluia!

LEADER: But Mary stood without at the sepulchre weeping, and she saw two angels. And they say unto her, woman why weepest thou? She saith, because they have taken away my Lord, and I know not where they have laid him. And she saw Jesus standing and knew not that it was Jesus. She, supposing him to be the gardener, saith unto him, Sir, if thou hast borne him hence, tell me where thou hast laid him. Jesus saith unto her, Mary. She turned herself and saith unto him, Master.

CONGREGATION: Alleluia!

LEADER: And behold, two of the disciples went that same day to a village called Emmaus, and they talked together of all these things which had happened. While they communed and reasoned, Jesus himself drew near and went with them.

CONGREGATION: Alleluia!

LEADER: When the doors were shut where the disciples were assembled, Jesus came and stood in the midst and saith unto them, peace be unto you. And when he had so said, he showed unto them his hands and his side.

CONGREGATION: Alleluia!

LEADER: Simon Peter saith unto the disciples, I go a-fishing. They say unto him, we also go with thee. And that night they caught nothing. But when the morning was now come, Jesus stood on the store, but the disciples knew not that it was Jesus. That disciple whom Jesus loved saith unto Peter, it is the Lord.

CONGREGATION: Alleluia!

LEADER: I was in the Spirit on the Lord's day and heard behind me a great voice as of a trumpet. And I turned to see the voice that spake with me. Being turned, I saw one like unto the Son of man, clothed with a garment down to the foot and girt about the breasts with a golden girdle. His hair was white as snow, and his feet like burnished brass, and his voice as the voice of many waters. And when I saw him, I fell at his feet as dead. And he laid his right hand upon me saying, fear not; I am the first and the last; I am he that liveth and was dead;

and behold, I am alive for evermore, and have the keys of hell and of death.

CONGREGATION: Alleluia! Alleluia! Alleluia![12]

✳ Benediction

LEADER: The Lord be with you.

CONGREGATION: And with you.

LEADER: Go and serve the Lord.

CONGREGATION: We will live as resurrection people.

LEADER: Begin a new life each day.

CONGREGATION: With Christ, every day is new.

ALL: Amen.

✳ Idea Starters

Hurray for God by John Buttrey, available from Contemporary Drama Service, is a good reading for Easter Sunday. Liturgical dance can be dramatically presented at an outdoor service. Plan an all-night vigil and make banners and other liturgical symbols for use at the sunrise service.

Thanksgiving

✳ Scripture Readings

> David's gratitude — 1 Chronicles 16:1–13
> A psalm of praise and thanksgiving — Psalm 92
> "Give thanks to the Lord" — Isaiah 12
> Jesus gives thanks — Matthew 15:32–39; 26:26–30
> Paul, the grateful Apostle — Corinthians 1:1–19, 15:50–58

✳ In Thankfulness
Poem

> One day for giving thanks; and yet the sun
> Sends abundant reassurance with each day
> Through all the year; and seeds select no one

Day's interval for growing want away
From earth; there is no stipulated hour
Alone of one brief season when eyes may see
The intricate slow opening of a flower
And the long rhythms of a wind-blown tree.
And since there are no set specific times
When birds wake sudden music from still air
And children's lilting laughter soars and climbs,
How shall we set a time for thankful prayer?
How shall we pay in one short interlude
Our year-long debt of joyous gratitude?

— **Jane Merchant**[13]

✳ For Thanksgiving
Responsive Reading

LEADER: Lord, when did we see you hungry?

CONGREGATION: We're thankful for the bread you gave to the multitudes. We're thankful for the body that was broken for us. We're grateful for the hungers that make us aware of our need of you. Make us aware that we are responsible for a hungry world.

LEADER: Lord, when did we see you thirsty?

CONGREGATION: We're thankful for that water that was made wine holding out a chance for all of us. We are thankful for the water of life you bring to us. We are grateful for the thirst that brings us to you.

LEADER: Lord, when did we see you a stranger?

CONGREGATION: We are thankful for your ministry to Zacchaeus and the Woman at the Well and Levi and Mary of Magdala. For while we were yet sinners you loved us. We are grateful for your church where we need not be strangers, but fellow citizens with the saints and members of the household of God.

LEADER: Lord, when did we see you naked?

CONGREGATION: We're thankful for the dignity of our faith. We thank you for the clothing you wrap around us. We thank you for the belief that all of us and each of us has a real worth. We are thankful that you take the prodigal back.

LEADER: Lord, when did we see you sick?

CONGREGATION: We are thankful that in our brokenness you came as Healer. That to our own ills you have come in healing love. We are thankful that the Great Physician is here.

LEADER: Lord, when did we see you in prison?

CONGREGATION: We are thankful that while we were yet afar off you came to set us free. We rejoice that we have freedom to move and to live and to find our uniqueness. We thank you for coming to us in our bondage and making us free.

— **Roger Lovette**[14]

❉ It Is Right to Give Thanks
Prayer

It is right to say Thanks to you, O God. That word wells up from deep inside us, for you have created us and the wonderful world in which we live. You are closer to us than the beating of our hearts, than the dreams of our minds. You provide the air we breathe, the food we eat, the ideas that prompt our best endeavors. We may ignore you. We may even deny you. But we depend upon you—so, Thanks! You will not let us alone. You come, insistently you come to us. Through apostles and prophets, through pastors and teachers, through parents and loving friends, you enter our lives. Through a Book you come to our minds. And especially in Jesus you have entered our history. Whenever we acknowledge your presence, we respond with words and acts of thanksgiving. It is the best thing that we can do. Amen.

— **J.M.B.**

Topical Resources

Youth Fellowship Occasions

In any group special occasions arise that need to be celebrated in a context of worship. Three ideas are given here: installation of officers, commissioning of persons to attend events in the larger church, and welcoming of new members.

Installation of New Officers

This service is designed to be used as an evening meeting of a youth fellowship. If a church prefers to recognize the new officers of the youth group by installing them during the Sunday morning worship service, the part headed "Service of Installation" may be lifted out. It is suggested that as symbols of their new responsibility, small pocket crosses made of oiled wood or light metal, available from denominational bookstores, may be given to the incoming officers.

✳ Call to Worship

From the rising of the sun to its setting the name of our God is to be praised.

✳ Hymn

"Joyful, Joyful We Adore Thee"

✳ Scripture Readings

(Choose one.)

Whom shall I send?—Isaiah 6:1–8
Follow me—Matthew 4:18–22
Go and make disciples of all nations—Matthew 28:16–20
Gifts that differ—Romans 12:4–8

✳ Follow the leader
Meditation

Do you remember the game you used to play as a child called "Follow the Leader," and how each player in turn was to mimic the antics or the skills of the one who was "It"? Tonight we are going to think about following the leader.

First, think a minute about the loyalty of the Old Testament prophets who followed the leading of God, knowing full well that they would pay the price of becoming unpopular with the mass of people to whom they preached. What would it have been like to have been one of them?   *(Keep silence for a time.)*

Now, think about the twelve men and those women who left their homes and ordinary occupations when Jesus went to them and said, "Follow me." What would it have been like to have been one of them? *(Keep silence for a time.)*

Think of the men and women who themselves were leaders in the early church, welcoming traveling Christians, perhaps hiding them, and always risking their own lives for their beliefs. What would it have been like to have been one of them?   *(Keep silence for a time.)*

All of us have been called to be leaders when we accepted the name of "Christian." But today, the risks are not nearly so great as they were before, at least not in the United States. It is good to remind ourselves at this time that leadership is not given lightly nor should it be accepted without a sense of dedication to the task.

Out of our own group we have now called a special few, who are to be our leaders for a period of time. We have given them special work to perform, and we know that God is expecting great things of them all. It is their responsibility to lead, and it is the responsibility of our group, which has elected them to their positions, to follow their leadership. But more than that, we all need to acknowledge our need to follow the leader who is Christ, who came that we might have life and have it abundantly.

✳ Act of Installation

LEADER: Jesus called forth from the multitudes that heard him, a few to be his disciples, and then he sent them forth to teach others to observe all that he had commanded them. Our youth fellowship, recognizing the need for leadership among our members, has called forth *(Name the new officers.)* from our membership to guide us in our deliberations, to preside at our meetings, and to lead us in all we do together. Will they please come forward. *(The new officers stand facing the group.)*

LEADER: My friends, these are your new officers for the coming *(Mention the length of their term.)* Do you accept their leadership and agree to follow it, accepting whatever responsibilities they in turn may ask of you?

GROUP: We do, God being our helper. *(The new officers turn and face the leader.)*

LEADER: You have heard your friends express their confidence in you as their new officers. Do you accept your new responsibilities and agree to do all in your power to make this fellowship a true community of Christians?

OFFICERS: We will, God being our helper.

LEADER: *(Presents pocket crosses to new officers.)* These pocket crosses are given to you as symbols of your new responsibilities as leaders of this group. May you ever be mindful of the stewardship of time and talent that your new office requires of you.

✳ God Has Chosen Some to Be Apostles
Prayer

Blessed be the name of God, who has chosen some to be apostles, some prophets, some evangelists, some pastors and teachers, some to follow and some to lead!

We pray, O God, that you bless these young people who have been chosen to serve as leaders and those who have pledged themselves to be faithful followers. May they all follow the leading of your spirit and may their fellowship be strengthened to do your will.

We ask your special favor upon these officers. Make them wise and faithful, humble and yet bold, constant, patient, and persevering in their appointed work. We ask this through the name of our one great leader, Jesus Christ. Amen.

* Hymn of Dedication:

"Take My Life and Let It Be"

* Benediction

And now may the God who has called us into service, guide us and guard us, this day and forevermore. Amen.

Commissioning Ceremony for Delegates to Youth Events, Conferences, or Camps

This ceremony is most appropriately used as a part of the Sunday morning worship service of the whole congregation. The leader could be the minister or other person representing the whole church.

* Act of Commissioning

The leader should begin by explaining the event(s) to which the persons are going and then, reading their names, call them forward.

LEADER: _____ Church is happy to commission you who will go as our representatives to _____.

DELEGATES: We are happy to receive your commission.

LEADER: You will soon go forth into a new adventure. We at home covet for you an opportunity to study and learn, so that you may grow in reverence for the good, the beautiful, and the true.

DELEGATES: We aspire to this as a part of our growth in the Christian life.

LEADER: We trust that the new friendships that you form will be a source of happiness during your stay, as well as an enrichment of your lives and the lives of others.

DELEGATES: We hope to find many new friends and to be true friends ourselves.

LEADER: We crave for you the companionship and influence of inspired teachers and the thrill of meeting and hearing great leaders in Christian work.

DELEGATES: We shall seek to learn more of the spirit of Christ.

LEADER: We hope you will return to us eager to share the visions you have seen and the inspiration you have received so that we who could not go with you may learn from you.

DELEGATES: We are eager to be of service to our church.

LEADER: We the members of _____ Church commission you as delegates to _____ .

✳ Speak to These Youth
Prayer

> Speak to these youth, O God, in the days ahead.
> Use each new experience, every new friendship,
> their songs and their laughter,
> the mealtimes and the late night conversations,
> to open their minds.
> Be with them in worship and in play.
> Show them a vision of a peaceful world
> in which no one goes hungry and all enjoy freedom and justice.
> Reveal to them the love of Jesus, in whose name we pray.
>
> — B.J.B.

✳ Hymn:

"Lord, Speak to Me"

A Service of Welcome to New Members

A single tall candle should be placed on the altar or a table at the front of the room. (This will be referred to as the Christ candle.) It should be surrounded by a circle of smaller candles for each officer and each new member. The Christ candle should be lighted before the service begins. The whole group should stand or sit in a circle or, if that is not possible, sit close together in rows.

✳ Call to Worship

LEADER: Remember your Creator in the days of your youth.

GROUP: "Ah, Lord God! Behold, I do not know how to speak, for I am only a youth."

LEADER: But the Lord said to me, "Do not say, 'I am only a youth': for to all to whom I send you you shall go, and whatever I command you you shall speak."

GROUP: "Here I am! Send me" (from Jeremiah and Isaiah).

✳ First Scripture Reading

Varieties of Gifts — 1 Corinthians 12:4–13

✳ Hymn Response

Lord, I want to be more loving
In my heart, in my heart;
Lord, I want to be more loving
In my heart.

✳ Second Scripture Reading

Many members — 1 Corinthians 12:14–26

✳ Hymn Response

Lord, I want to be more holy
In my heart, in my heart;
Lord, I want to be more holy
In my heart.

✳ Third Scripture Reading

Members of the Body of Christ — 1 Corinthians 12:27–31

✳ Hymn Response

Lord, I want to be a Christian
In my heart, in my heart;
Lord, I want to be a Christian
In my heart.

✳ Giving the Peace

(Choose a way to say "The peace of God be with you" to one another that will
have meaning within your group. A group in a circle can hold hands and pass
the words around squeezing hands; large groups may want just to greet those
around them. If there is a particular custom in your church, you will want to
follow it.)

✳ Candlelighting Ceremony of Welcome

LEADER: Will the new members of this fellowship and the officers please rise and come forward. *(The group should either come to the front or form a smaller circle inside the larger one.)*

With the Giving of the Peace we have sealed the bonds of community and have affirmed that although we are many, we are "members one of another." Hereafter as one member sorrows, all sorrow also. When one member rejoices, all join in the gladness.

We are also called to let our light so shine that those who see it may give glory to God. Our welcome to you will be complete when, symbolically, we share with you the light that has come into our lives through Christ. I light my candle from the Christ candle and pass the light to the officers of the group. Through them the light is passed to you.

(Here the leader lights each of the small unlighted candles from the Christ candle and hands them to each of the officers. The new memers are given unlighted candles, and at a signal, officers light the new members' candles.)

✳ Benediction

LEADER: May the light which shone in the darkness in the life and death and resurrection of our Lord now burn in your hearts, that you in turn may let that light shine through you upon others.

RESPONSE: *(sung softly)*
Lord, I want to be like Jesus
In my heart, in my heart;
Lord, I want to be like Jesus,
In my heart.
In my heart, in my heart,
Lord, I want to be like Jesus
In my heart.

Peace and Justice

The biblical term Shalom is sometimes translated into English as "peace," but the word Shalom means much more than just the absence of war. It includes the concepts of wholeness and harmony, of well-being and unity, and of justice for all people. In our own concerns for peace and justice we often separate out specific issues such as hunger, nuclear energy, or racism, but when we look deeper we find the issues are intertwined. For that reason these resources on peace and justice are grouped together in one section.

A globe or map of the world along with the cross could be used as visual aids in worship. Other symbols might include the United Nations or World Council of Churches logo or the peace symbol. Projected slides of a nuclear cloud or faces of hungry people are another possibility along with appropriate posters or banners.

✳ Scripture Readings

The call to serve others — Isaiah 61:1–4
Let justice roll down like waters — Amos 5:21–24
Beat swords into plowshares — Micah 4:1–4
Love your enemies — Matthew 5:43–48; Luke 6:27–31
The great commandment — Matthew 22:35 — 40
I was hungry and you fed me — Matthew 25:35–40
The Good Samaritan — Luke 10:25–37.

✳ Hymns and Other Music

"God, the Omnipotent"
"Where Cross the Crowded Ways of Life"
"In Christ There Is No East or West"
"God of Grace and God of Glory"
"When I Needed a Neighbor"
"Ain't Gonna Study War No More"
"Let There Be Peace on Earth"
"I've Got Peace Like a River"
"Blowing in the Wind"
"We Shall Overcome"
"Shalom Chaverim"
"From the Slave Pens of the Delta"

✳ Francis — The Peace-Loving Saint
Meditation

Eight hundred years ago, a son was born to the Italian cloth merchant Pietro di Bernadone and the noble Lady Pica in the feudal town of Assisi. Francesco, as the boy was known, was still a teenager when the people of his town rose up in revolt and overthrew their feudal lords, making Assisi one of the few free cities of that time.

At first a good member of the middle class, Francesco was a merchant like his father. But when he was in his early twenties he began to change. He saw that the values by which he was ordering his life, which were those of his father and of most of society, were not God's values. It was not an overnight conversion, but Francesco decided that more than anything else, he wanted to live the gospel of Jesus Christ. Since Jesus had said, "Sell everything you have and distribute to the poor" (Luke 18:22), Francesco tried to do just that. But when the goods he sold came from his father's shop, there was a public scene! Pietro hauled his son before the authorities, and there Francesco stripped himself of everything he had — entrusting his life to God in heaven. He moved into an abandoned church outside the city and began to discover what a "gospel life" was all about.

Francesco spent the rest of his life, until he died worn out at the age of 46, trying to live the gospel. Early on in his new life, as he later put it, the Lord gave him some brothers — other young men inspired by what he was doing. By 1209 he had a dozen followers, and needed to organize his group into a more structured religious community. Only seven years later, a French bishop named Jacques de Vitry wrote home from the Middle East, where he had journeyed with some Crusaders: "In the midst of this corruption I nonetheless found consolation in seeing a great number of men and women who renounced all their possessions for the love of Christ; 'Lesser Brothers' and 'Lesser Sisters' as they were called." Francesco always wanted to be considered the least important and the servant of all.

In a society torn apart by constant warfare, Francesco was a radical; he went to the root of the problem. Since it was customary for adults to carry around a sword or a knife (there were robbers on nearly every highway), Francesco and his followers made a bold move. Instead of the usual leather belt, they wore a knotted rope around their waists — on which it was impossible to carry a sword.

Today, Francesco di Pietro di Bernadone is better known as Saint Francis of Assisi. The Franciscan Movement he began numbers hundreds of thousands of men and women all over the world. There are Lesser Brothers and Sisters, as well as Poor Clares (as the "Poor Ladies of Assisi" are commonly known) and Secular Franciscans (the Third Order) in the Roman Catholic, Anglican, and Lutheran communities. Eight hundred years later, Francis' dream is carried on by everyone who genuinely tries to live the gospel of Jesus.

— **Bill Barrett, O.F.M.**[15]

✳ Lord, Make Me a Channel of Thy Peace

A Prayer of Francis of Assisi
(This prayer is arranged for a choric speech choir, divided into three groups with varying voice pitches. Group 1 has the highest voices and Group 3 the lowest.

The entire group will find it helpful to discuss the text line by line until everyone has a general understanding of the prayer and its meaning. Then their reading and speaking of it will follow more naturally.

In the first part of this prayer, Group 2 should speak rather softly, providing a background accompaniment. They pick up their rhythm from Group 1, being careful to speak immediately after Group 1. Group 3 should come in before Group 2 has completely finished. Experiment will lead to the best timing of voices.)

ALL: Lord, make me a channel of thy peace.

GROUP 1: That where there is hatred —

GROUP 2: (no hatred, no hatred, no hatred)

GROUP 3: I may bring love.

GROUP 1: That where there is wrong —

GROUP 2: (no wrong, no wrong, no wrong)

GROUP 3: I may bring the spirit of forgiveness.

GROUP 1: That where there is discord —

GROUP 2: (no discord, no discord, no discord)

GROUP 3: I may bring harmony.

GROUP 1: That where there is error —

GROUP 2: (no error, no error, no error)

GROUP 3: I may bring truth.

GROUP 1: That where there is doubt —

GROUP 2: (no doubt, no doubt, no doubt)

GROUP 3: I may bring faith

GROUP 1: That where there is despair —

GROUP 2: (no despair, no despair, no despair)

GROUP 3: I may bring hope.

GROUP 1: That where there are shadows —

GROUP 2: (no shadows, no shadows, no shadows)

GROUP 3: I may bring light.

GROUP 1: Lord, grant that I may seek rather to comfort, than to be comforted.

GROUP 2 AND 3: To understand, than to *be* understood.

ALL: To love, than to be loved.
Lord, make me a channel of thy peace!
— **Francis of Assisi,** arranged by Barbara Fuchs[16]

✳ I Have a Dream
Meditation

Martin Luther King, Jr., had the remarkable ability not only to inspire thousands of black and white Americans to risk their lives for justice but also to persuade the nation that the time had come to fulfill its vision of freedom for all.

During the 1963 March on Washington for Jobs and Freedom, the Atlanta Baptist minister gave a stirring speech that caught the imagination of more than 200,000 people who gathered at the Lincoln Memorial. Millions more watched on television as the civil rights leader—with the superb timing of a black preacher—prompted an enthusiastic response from the vast crowd each time he uttered the words, "I have a dream." His speech is reprinted in *Drum Majors for Justice,* edited by Ruth L. Sprague (New York: United Church Press, 1970).

✳ Litany for a Hungry World

LEADER: "Give us this day our daily bread (Matt. 6:11)."

GROUP: Yes, Lord, you have taught us to pray for bread. You aren't so "spiritual" as some of the people who use your name. You know that we are flesh and blood, that we need food, that hunger hurts, that we can find joy and strength in eating.

LEADER: "You shall not live by bread alone (Matt. 4:4, from Deut. 8:3)."

GROUP: You have told us — and life has taught us — that we live by bread, but not by bread alone. Food can mean greed, oppression, overindulgence. Food can be a bribe, a threat, a means of manipulation. Food shared is an expression of our common humanity and of love. O God, creator of the world and of us, let us use your gifts of food as a blessing to this human race.

LEADER: "The laborer deserves food (Matt. 10:10)."

GROUP: But some cannot find work. Others work but cannot earn enough food for themselves and their children. God of justice and mercy, move within us to change our society so that people may work, eat, and share the world's plenty and need.

LEADER: "I was hungry and you gave me food, I was thirsty and you gave me drink (Matt. 25:35)."

GROUP: We often say we are hungry. Maybe we even say that we are about to starve. But how little we know about hunger! We skip a meal and call it hunger. But real hunger means pain, gnawing pain, relentless pain. It means weariness and weakness. It means sickness and death. O God, if we are ever really hungry, may someone give us food. O God, may we, now, find ways to feed the hungry and to empower them to feed themselves.

LEADER: "Taking the five loaves and the two fish he looked up to heaven, and blessed, and broke and gave the loaves to the disciples, and the disciples gave them to the crowds (Matt. 14:19)."

GROUP: God of love, we know that shared food will go farther than we usually think. If we care enough, it will go around the world. Shake us, trouble us, strengthen us to share.

LEADER: "The Lord Jesus on the night when he was betrayed took bread, and when he had given thanks, he broke it, and said, 'This is my body which is for you (1 Cor. 11:23–24).' "

GROUP: We meet you, Creator God, in prayer. We meet you in exalted moments. But in the supreme sacrament of our faith, we meet you in eating. You have blessed eating, ennobled it, turned its necessity to joyful privilege. When we eat, let us remember—sometimes at least—that you are with us and that your gift of food is your gift of yourself.

LEADER: "He was known to them in the breaking of the bread (Luke 24:35)."

GROUP: "Let us break bread together on our knees; let us break bread together on our knees. When I fall on my knees, with my face to the rising sun, O Lord, have mercy on me."

— Roger L. Shinn[17]

✳ Litany for Peace With Justice

LEADER: We long for homes which are safe places of rest and security, a base from which we can reach out to others, but we sometimes fail in generosity and justice toward family members and the homeless.

PEOPLE: Holy God, fill our hearts with justice and peace.

LEADER: We long for communities where people have adequate access to food, clothing, shelter, education, employment, and social relationships, but we experience conflicts in our values and choices.

PEOPLE: Holy God, fill our hearts with justice and peace.

LEADER: We long for a nation which is unified in God, where every man, woman, and child experiences liberty in their lives and justice in having basic human needs met, yet we are often separated into the "haves" and "have nots."

PEOPLE: Holy God, fill our hearts with justice and peace.

LEADER: We long for a world where we all recognize one another as brothers and sisters, where we can resolve our conflicts and the unequal distribution of wealth with justice and peace.

ALL: Holy God, fill our hearts with justice and peace.

— **Peace With Justice Week**[18]

✳ Community Affirmation

We, who live in the shadow of the mushroom cloud,
We, whose very bones and lungs are threatened even now by radioactivity,
Today declare our hope in the future.

From the diversity of our religious traditions,
We have come to renew our belief in the holiness of the earth and the sanctity of all life.

We declare we are at peace with all people of good will.
We need no leader to define for us any enemy,
Nor to tell us what we need security for and defense against.

Instead, we affirm that our earth's security rests not in armaments, but
In the justice of adequate housing and food,
In the justice of meaningful education and work,
In the justice of an economic order that gives everyone access to our earth's abundance,
In the justice of human relationships, nourished by cooperation,
In the justice of safe, clean and renewable energy, instead of the perils of nuclear power.

We affirm people over property, community over privatism,
Respect for others regardless of sex, race or class.

We choose struggle rather than indifference,
We choose to be friends of the earth and of one another, rather than exploiters.
We choose to be citizens rather than subjects,
We choose to be peacemakers rather than peacekeepers,
We choose a nuclear-free future,
And we will settle for nothing less.

We unite ourselves with sisters and brothers the world over,
To join together in communities of resistance to the nuclear threat.
We unite ourselves with trust in the Spirit of Life;
Justice and love can overcome the machines of destruction.

Before us today are set life and death,
We choose life, that we and our children may live.
Let it be so.

— **Peace With Justice Week**[19]

✳ In Your Hands We Lay the World

O God of peace,
In your hands
  we lay the giants of this world;
In your hands
  we lay the black and the white,
    the rich and the poor,
    the young and the old;
In your hands
  we lay India and Pakistan,
    North and South Vietnam,
    Egypt and Israel,
    America and Russia;
In your hands
  we lay China,
    all the nations that try to develop,
    and all the nations that are developed.
All the gaps—we lay in your hands.

Help us
  to build bridges and not widen the distances any further,
  to demask giants and not blow them up any bigger,
  to look realities in the face
    and not shut them out from confrontation.
Help us
  to choose between the right and the wrong things to do;
    between going along with or being opposed to
      what our government, our society, our community, our
      schools are doing;
  to choose between the draft and conscientious objection;
  to participate critically and be real salt
    instead of sugar.

Enlighten our minds,
Give us vision,
Make us creative.
Help us struggle.
   for the sake of the world, your world,
   the one world you promised us,

— **Annemarth van Lelyfeld**[20]

✳ A Peace Prayer

Lead me from death to life,
   from falsehood to truth.
Lead me from despair to hope,
   from fear to trust.
Lead me from hate to love,
   from war to peace.
Let peace fill our heart, our world,
   our universe. Amen.[21]

✳ Voices From Private Worlds
Responsive reading for two groups

THE VOICES: There is one great world in which all people share a common existence; but there are millions of tiny private worlds, in each of which single human beings think and feel and have their being. In our private worlds, we fight our fiercest battles, win our brightest victories, and sometimes, lost in the valley of fears, we stand trembling alone in the dark. We speak to you from some of the private worlds that lie within the varieties of humanity. We want to reach you, and we want to be reached, but often you seem far away and the distance between us is cold. Will you try to understand?

PEOPLE OF THE CHURCH: We will try to understand. We, too, have private worlds, and we know the desolation of holding our hands to empty air. Who are you?

THE VOICES: We are the blind, who live in worlds without color. We cannot see the splendor of summer blossoms, or spinning snow, or the face of our pastor praying in the sanctuary. But sometimes, in the beauty of sudden knowledge, we have seen the face of God, and we know that it is kind. God has given us many roads to fulfillment. May we follow them with you?

PEOPLE OF THE CHURCH: We will share with you our laughter, which you can hear, our hymns, which you can sing, and every task to which your hands bring skill. We will not shut you out.

THE VOICES: We are the deaf, who do not hear your songs. But we can see your faces when they smile and your hands when they are outstretched, and the opening door of the house of God. May we come in and serve with you?

PEOPLE OF THE CHURCH: The door that God has opened is for everyone. Your worship and your gifts will bless us.

THE VOICES: We are those of crippled limbs and twisted bodies. But in our private worlds our spirits stand straight and tall. Let us show you the stride of our minds and hearts.

PEOPLE OF THE CHURCH: The race of life is to the strong of spirit. Be our pacemakers and blaze the trail.

THE VOICES: We live in the worlds of shame. We are the alcoholics, the drug addicts, the prisoners. Our eyes fall before you, and we dare not ask you to be our friends.

PEOPLE OF THE CHURCH: You need not ask, for we accept you without petition. We are not the good people, sitting in judgment on the weak. We are only seekers after goodness, who sin and fall and rise again, through the grace of God. Your worlds are harsher than ours, and so your struggles are more grievous. But we see in you a sharpened image of ourselves. Come with us to the altar and let us pray together: "God, give us courage."

THE VOICES: We are the aged, who live in the world that you will inhabit tomorrow. These are strange worlds, not like the shining stars on which we lived when we were young. Sometimes we stumble on the trails and call to the Guide to show us the turning. And often we cry to you in our hearts. Do you hear us?

PEOPLE OF THE CHURCH: Perhaps we have not always heard, but we will try not to fail you again. For you are the selves we soon will be. And we are the selves you once have been. Our spirits cannot be divided.

THE VOICES: We are many others. We are those people everywhere who live in the stormy private worlds, the worlds of those who are hurt in body, or mind, or spirit.

PEOPLE OF THE CHURCH: But who is not hurt? Who has not been broken?

THE VOICES: Give us the care that we require, and take from us the gifts we offer, for we need both compassion and praise.

PEOPLE OF THE CHURCH: We will give to you, in God's Name.

THE VOICES: We will take from you, in God's Name.

PEOPLE OF THE CHURCH: We will ask from you, in God's Name, not for your sake alone, but because we need you, too.

THE VOICES: And we will respond, to complete the fellowship.

BOTH GROUPS TOGETHER: The distance between private worlds is like the space between planets, and only through God's grace can we cross the awful boundaries. But in God's plan all things are possible, God has given us the chart for the journey; God has marked the course we must follow; and the name of the way is Love.

— Adapted from **Mae Hurley Ashworth**[27]

✳ Fasting for Peace and Justice
Responsive meditation

The responsive reading that follows, based on the prophecy of Isaiah (Is. 58:1–12 [TEV]), describes how the lovers of peace and justice are to practice fasting. The group may be divided into two sections to alternate reading. The responsive lesson is followed by a responsive prayer that incorporates the Greek words *Kyrie Eleison*, which mean "Lord, have mercy." The *Kyrie* may either be spoken or sung to any of several traditional settings. An especially popular musical setting, from the liturgy of the Russian Orthodox Church, appears on page 191.

RIGHT: The Lord says, "Shout as loud as you can! Tell my people Israel about their sins! They worship me every day, claiming that they are eager to know my ways and obey my laws. They say they want me to give them just laws and that they take pleasure in worshiping me."

LEFT: The people ask, "Why should we fast if the Lord never notices? Why should we go without food if God pays no attention?"

RIGHT: The Lord says to them, "The truth is that at the same time you fast, you pursue your own interests and oppress your workers."

LEFT: Your fasting makes you violent, and you quarrel and fight. Do you think this kind of fasting will make me listen to your prayers?

RIGHT: When you fast, you make yourselves suffer; you bow your heads low like a blade of grass and spread out sackcloth and ashes to lie on. Is that what you call fasting? Do you think I will be pleased with that?

LEFT: The kind of fasting I want is this: Remove the chains of oppression and the yoke of injustice, and let the oppressed go free.

RIGHT: Share your food with the hungry and open your homes to the homeless poor.

LEFT: Give clothes to those who have nothing to wear, and do not refuse to help your own relatives.

RIGHT: Then my favor will shine on you like the morning sun, and your wounds will be quickly healed.

LEFT: I will always be with you to save you; my presence will protect you on every side.

RIGHT: When you pray, I will answer you. When you call to me, I will respond.

LEFT: If you put an end to oppression, to every gesture of contempt, and to every evil word;

RIGHT: If you give food to the hungry and satisfy those who are in need, then the darkness around you will turn to the brightness of noon. And I will always guide you and satisfy you with good things.

LEFT: I will keep you strong and well. You will be like a garden that has plenty of water, like a spring of water that never goes dry.

ALL: Your people will rebuild what has long been in ruins, building again on the old foundations. You will be known as the people who rebuilt the walls, who restored the ruined houses.

LEADER: For freedom Christ has set us free; stand fast therefore and do not submit again to a yoke of slavery.

PEOPLE: Gracious God, our hearts are heavy as we acknowledge the injustice, oppression and suffering in our world.
We remember before you all those who are victims of unjust systems, all those who are crushed by forces of oppression, robbed of rights and dignity, treated as objects and not as people made in your own image;
all those who are hungry, homeless, and without the necessities of daily life;
all those who are tortured, imprisoned, persecuted and put to death;
all those who are broken in body, mind, or spirit. . . .

LEADER: Lord, God of justice and peace, comfort those who suffer from violence and war; strengthen those who work for peace,

guide those who make decisions for the nations. . . .
Help us to hammer our swords into ploughs, our spears into pruning-knives.

ALL: Kyrie Eleison

PEOPLE: Loving God, you have called us to be one, to live in unity and harmony, and yet we are divided:

> race from race,
> faith from faith,
> church from church,
> rich from poor,
> old from young,
> sick from healthy,
> neighbor from neighbor. . . .

LEADER: O Lord, by whose cross all enmity is brought to an end,
break down the walls that separate us,
tear down the fences of hatred and indifference,
forgive us for the sins that divide us,
free us from pride and self-seeking, overcome our prejudices and fears,
give us courage to open ourselves to others; by the power of your Spirit set us free, make us one, empower us to serve.

ALL: Kyrie Eleison

LEADER: Sisters and Brothers,
let us claim the freedom Christ gives.
May Christ empower us to serve together in faith, hope and love.
Go in peace to love and serve the Lord.

PEOPLE: In the name of Christ. Amen.[23]

✳ Idea Starters

Study the scripture lessons in this section and think of ways to relate the biblical message to the headlines in today's newspaper. But remember that although services should have a theme, worship is more than a topical program.

Arrange for special services on such national holidays as Martin Luther King's Birthday, Presidents' Day, Memorial Day, Independence Day, Labor Day, and Veterans' Day. The service might be in the morning before school or in the evening. Or you might suggest that the youth group participate in the Sunday morning service of worship on the Sunday before such holidays.

Discuss patriotism and world peace, and plan a service before school on October 24, the anniversary of the founding of the United Nations. Or hold an ecumenical youth event on the Sunday nearest United Nations' Day.

The Church: Unity and Mission

Although there are (and always have been) a few Christians who devote themselves to prayer and the simple life as hermits, most Christians want and need an organization to help them express their faith. Since the first century, that organization has been called the church. It may be structured in different ways. Some are monarchies headed by a pope, a patriarch, or bishops. Others are governed by representatives or place the power in each congregation. But all of them meet regularly for the same purpose: to worship God by singing psalms and hymns, reading scripture, and proclaiming the Word through preaching; most of them celebrate at least two sacraments.

From the earliest days when Christians met in the catacombs and in private houses, they expressed thanksgiving that they could be together and prayed for other Christians in other times and places. It is therefore natural to plan services of worship to recognize the church.

✳ Scripture Readings

> One body, many members — Romans 12:1–8
> One Lord, one faith, one baptism — Ephesians 4:1–8
> The body of Christ — 1 Corinthians 12:27–31
> The Lord's anointed — Isaiah 61:1–3 or Luke 4:14–19
> The salt of the earth — Matthew 5:13–16
> The great commission — Matthew 28:16–20
> The Good Shepherd — John 10:14–16
> Disciples first called Christians — Acts 11:19–26
> Paul, Apostle to Gentiles — Acts 13:44–49
> A missionary letter — Colossians 1:1–8
> The birth of the church — Acts 2

✳ Lord of Springtime and Harvest
Prayer

O God, thou Lord of springtime and harvest, we beseech thee to bless the seed sown throughout the world for the sustenance of humankind. So water it with the gentle rain from heaven and warm it with the golden sunshine that it may bear fruit a hundredfold, to the glory of thy holy name and the welfare of thy people; through Jesus Christ our Lord. Amen.

— Rural Life Prayers[24]

✳ Made of One Blood
Prayer

Almighty God, who hast made of one blood all nations of men for to dwell on the face of the earth, remind us in this hour that we are but one part of a vast fellowship. Turn our thoughts outward and help us to feel a closer communion with thy whole church. Amen.

— Traditional (adapted)

✳ In Thee We Are United
Prayer

> Lord God, in thee we are united.
> Before thee there are no great or small, none inferior — none
>   superior.
> But all are members together of thy Holy Body.
> In the least of thy friends, thou dost confront us.
> Lord, let us be grounded steadfastly in thy holy community.
> Fill our hearts with the strength and joy of thy love.
> May we — pilgrims — find a home with thee.
> Take thou from us the pain of division, the fear in the souls of
>   those who stand alone.
> Unite us in the temple thou art building — thy church.
> There we shall be thy people forever and ever. Amen.

— Karl Bernard Ritter[25]

✳ Invocation

LEADER: Come from the east and the west,
    from the north and the south,
    and worship the God of our mothers and fathers,
    the God of Jesus Christ.

PEOPLE: Amen.

LEADER: The grace of our Lord Jesus Christ and the love of God and
    the communion of the Holy spirit be with you all.

PEOPLE: And also with you.[26]

✴ Doxology

Praise God from whom all blessings flow;
Praise Christ the Word in flesh born low;
Praise Holy Spirit evermore;
One God, Triune, whom we adore.

Through north and south and east and west,
May God's immortal Name be blest;
Till every-where beneath the sun
God's peace shall reign,
God's will be done. Amen.[27]

✴ Commissioning

LEADER: Let us go forth into the world in the name of Jesus Christ, the
Word of Life. By the power of the Holy Spirit, let us remain
faithful to God's will in the streets, our homes, and our places
of labor and leisure;

PEOPLE: That whether we are gathered or scattered we may be the
servant church of the servant Christ, who bids us anew, "Take
up your cross and follow me."[28]

✴ Blessing

May the God of Sarah and Abraham bless you.
May God the Son, Jesus Christ, born of our sister Mary, bless
you.
May God the Holy Spirit, who broods over us as parents brood
over their children, bless you.[29]

✴ Confession of Sin

LEADER: In gathering to praise God, we remember that we have
preferred our wills to God's will. Accepting God's power to
make us a new creation in Christ, let us ask God to forgive us.

PEOPLE: Eternal God, our judge and redeemer,
You call us to be one holy people
and send us to serve you in a broken and divided world.
But we separate ourselves from each other.
Pride hinders our obedience.

We fail to show your presence in our lives.
We are indifferent to those in need around us.
Lord, have mercy upon us,
cleanse us from our sins,
and heal our brokenness
that we may henceforth serve you in newness of life,
to the glory of your holy name.
(The people may pray silently.)[30]

✳ Declaration of Pardon

LEADER: Hear the good news!
The saying is sure and worthy of full acceptance, that Christ Jesus came into the world to save sinners.
Friends, believe the good news of the gospel.

PEOPLE: In Jesus Christ, we are forgiven.

LEADER: The peace of the Lord Jesus Christ be with you all.

PEOPLE: And also with you.
(All may greet one another in the name of the Lord, saying, "Peace be with you.")[31]

✳ A Litany for Unity

LEADER: Merciful God, who didst name thy Son Jesus, that he should save his people from their sins,

PEOPLE: Forgive and heal our divisions.

LEADER: Good Shepherd, who wilt gather all thy sheep in one fold, so there will be one flock,

PEOPLE: Unite us in thy truth.

LEADER: Spirit of God, who dost bestow diversities of gifts upon thy people for the edification of all,

PEOPLE: Maintain our unity in the bond of peace.

ALL: Father, Son, and Holy Spirit, one God everlasting, forgive and heal our divisions, unite us in thy truth, maintain our unity in the bond of peace. Amen.[32]

✳ A Litany for Rural People

LEADER: O God, Creator and lover of all: that it may please thee to bless all those who sow the seed and reap the harvests of the world;

PEOPLE: We beseech thee to hear us.

LEADER: That it may please thee to bless all those who service and repair our farm machines, that they fail not at planting time;

PEOPLE: We beseech thee to hear us.

LEADER: That thy pastors so minister among the people that they instill into the hearts of all who labor a sense of the worth of their toil;

PEOPLE: We beeseech thee to hear us.

LEADER: That it may please thee to bless the homes and home life of our country districts, that they may be pure and happy abiding places for the children that shall come to them;

PEOPLE: We beseech thee to hear us.

LEADER: That people living in country districts may realize the great part they may play in the church's work in the world and consecrate themselves to thy worship and to service of others;

PEOPLE: We beseech thee to hear us, O Lord.

ALL: O God of all creation, we beseech thee to bless all those who through thy church seek to serve thee in the rural areas of the world. Help them in their efforts to sow the seed of thy kingdom, and when the harvest seems meager or far off, confirm thy promise to them and make them believe that in due season they shall reap if they faint not; through Jesus Christ our Lord. Amen.

— E. W. Mueller[33]

Pentecost: The Birthday of the Church

Christians celebrate Pentecost (or Whitsunday) as the birthday of the church. From the small but exciting beginning described in Acts 2, the church has spread around the world. Today it is a force for uniting a badly divided world. Three traditional forms of prayer are provided in the material that follows: a confession to be used privately or spoken in unison, a short "collect" that can be read by the leader or by the group in unison, and a litany, or responsive prayer. Any of the hymns of the church or the two printed in this section could be appropriately used at Pentecost.

✳ Prayer of Confession

O Thou whose word dost silence all our tongues and cause all the peoples of the earth to tremble: hear our confusions and our confession for we are body broken and beyond belief. The eyes thou hast given us to behold thy glory, we have averted to avoid thy light. The arms thou hast given us to hold close our neighbor, we have folded forever in distrust. The tongues thou hast given us to proclaim thy wisdom, we have employed to show forth our foolishness. The church thou hast given us as a sign of thy love, we have silenced lest it suggest a greater truth than our own.

O Word made flesh, we lay before thee the babel of this day: the empty agreements, the prattling politics, the endless bargains to preserve our power in the name of peace. We are people who prefer the sound of superiority to the still voice of thy saving grace.

Enter even now our trembling hearts and heal our manifold divisions. As thou didst give birth to thy church with tongues of fire, so shake us back to life with the rush of thy wind and the wonder of thy Word. Leave us not to our own devices for we shall surely perish. But call us to such a repentance that the world will bow down not before its arsenals but be held at long last in thine everlasting arms. Through Jesus Christ our Lord.

Amen.

✳ Collect

O Holy Spirit who art always invading our forsaken spaces and dost find us forever in need of thy fire and thy forgiveness,

Find us even now gathered and yet gone astray. Silence every sound but thine own until the peace which passes understanding plays havoc with our politics and bends our pride to thy control through Jesus Christ our Lord.

Amen.

✳ Prayers of the People

LEADER: O Lord of all time yet beyond time, God of the vast universe and very God of our most intimate geography, keeper of the world we know and promiser of a kingdom we barely can imagine, we give thee thanks for life itself; for birth that signals the advent of our hope and death that reminds us how precarious and precious and fragile is our every moment; for seconds that seem like eternity yet elude our grasp, and for eternity that invades every day of our lives and engages us in the actions of hope, in the acrobatics of peace, in the absurdities of love.

PEOPLE: O God, invade this time with thy Holy Spirit.

LEADER: Thanks be to thee for time that connects us with this temporal globe of boundaries that are bound to shift, and rulers who collapse daily and the peoples who endure in spite of all that threatens to undo them.

PEOPLE: O God, enter this globe like the rush of a mighty wind.

LEADER: We pray for the world of this time, O Most High and Holy One, though we know not what to pray. In the wisdom of thy timelessness, if it be thy will, let the powerful be provoked into silence and the powerless remember thy faithfulness to all generations.

PEOPLE: O God, come to us with tongues of fire.

LEADER: Let terrorists attempt even tenderness and convert communists and capitalists alike to acts of compassion; let there be largeness of heart in Israel and patience among Palestinians and tolerance in Egypt; let the hurt of thy people in Ireland for once be healed and keep El Salvador from slaughtering itself; let there be solidarity in Poland and some semblance of justice in South Africa; and in this great nation, O Lord, confound the politicians until they be makers of peace.

PEOPLE: O God, invade this time with thy Holy Spirit.

LEADER: O God, for thy timeless self-touching, anguishing, persuading, patiently exposing our very being into life and life eternal, we give thee thanks, now and forever. Amen.[36]

The Unity of the Church

✳ An Affirmation of the Unity of Christ's Church

LEADER: Let us say what we believe.

PEOPLE: We believe
       that it is God's creative intention that the world live as one.

that Christ's prayer for the unity of the Church express his
abiding will.
that the Holy Spirit's activity is reconciliation and peace.

We acknowledge
that we suffer from disunity within our denominations,
that we are impoverished by our separation from other
churches,
that pride and fear inhibit our search for unity.

We are confident
that the Church even now is one in the Holy Spirit,
that Jesus Christ is the center of the Church's unity,
that the Spirit is working toward the day when we shall be
visibly one in Christ.

We proclaim
that God wills all humanity to be one,
that the Church's unity is a sign and means of the unity of
humankind.

We covenant
to open our eyes and ears to the reconciling Word of God,
to open our hearts to gifts which the Spirit would give us
through others,
to open our churches to experiences of unity in each place
and all places.

We move forward
prepared to live with the uncertainty of new directions,
prepared to die to all that keeps us apart,
prepared to be resurrected as one with all people in
Christ.[37]

✳ The Unity of the Church
Meditation

When you travel abroad, you are often asked what your nationality is.
Unless you are hopelessly provincial, you would not answer, "I am a
Missourian," or "I am a North Dakotan." You would reply, "I am an
American." Your identity as a member of the whole nation is more
important than your specific location within the nation or the peculiar
characteristics of the locality where you live.

It is equally strange when you are asked what your religious faith is to answer, "I am a Presbyterian," or "I am a Methodist." The correct answer is, "I am a Christian." Often you hear someone describing another by saying, "He is one of the Baptist faith," or "She was reared in the Lutheran faith." Such statements are basically incorrect. There is only the *Christian* faith. True faith in Christ is exactly the same thing whether you are a Quaker, an Anglo-Catholic, or a member of the United Church of Christ. Your relation to Christ is quite above the particular denomination to which you belong.

— **Donald G. Miller**[38]

✳ The Church in the City
Meditation

(Introduce this meditation by announcing that before beginning you would like the group to turn to the hymn "Where Cross the Crowded Ways of Life" in the hymnal. After each scripture reading the group is to respond by singing one stanza of the hymn.)

Frank Mason North knew the city well, for he had city parishes and spent many years working for the New York City Mission and Church Extension Society. Shortly after preaching a sermon on the text, "Go ye therefore into the partings of the highways" (Matt. 22:9, American Standard Version), he was caught up in the idea and wrote the hymn "Where Cross the Crowded Ways of Life."

The words of this hymn became a symbol to many Christians of the church ministering to the big city, and they have been carved on the side of a large church that stands at the intersection of two major streets in the city of St. Louis, for all passers-by to see and remember.

Let us take time now to consider carefully what the words of Dr. North's hymn mean, coupling each stanza with a related passage of scripture.

(Leader reads Matthew 23:37–39.)
(Group sings stanza 1 of "Where Cross the Crowded Ways of Life.")

LEADER: Matthew 8:14–7

GROUP: Stanza 2 of the hymn

LEADER: Matthew 9:10–13

GROUP: Stanza 3

LEADER: Matthew 25:35–40

GROUP: Stanza 4

LEADER: Matthew 8:1–3

GROUP: Stanza 5

LEADER: 1 John 4:16, 20–21

GROUP: Stanza 6

(At the conclusion the entire hymn may be sung softly, as a prayer.)

✳ God's Whole Church
Responsive Meditation

LEADER: And Jesus said, "You are Peter, and upon this rock I will build my church."

GROUP: "And the gates of hell will not prevail against it."

LEADER: Because I love little country churches, hid among elms and birches, crying babes in arms, preachers unalarmed.

GROUP: I love your kingdom, Lord, the house of your abode.

LEADER: I love city churches: inner-city churches, pointing ever to past accomplishments; yearning, hoping for a better day.

GROUP: The church our blest Redeemer saved with his own blood.

LEADER: I love black churches, with solid preaching, rousing music, handclapping; endless rounds of Amens and Hallelujahs.

GROUP: I love your Church, O God! Her walls before you stand.

LEADER: I love Catholic churches: stately spires with traditional crosses pointing heavenward; odors of incense and candles burning.

GROUP: Dear as the apple of your eye, and graven on your hand.

LEADER: I love mission churches in mushrooming areas at home or deep in Africa or Asia—telling of Christ, often making little headway.

GROUP: For her my tears shall fall, for her my prayers ascend.

LEADER: I love house churches: people seated on carpeted floors, coffee cups rattling; with the sincere seeking and searching out new ways.

GROUP: To her my cares and toils be given, till toils and cares shall end.

LEADER: I love Quaker churches; a respite from much talking with periods of deep meditation; and occasional headnodding; Holy Spirit moving.

GROUP: Beyond my highest joy, I praise her heavenly ways.

LEADER: I love denominational churches: members often confused as to ownership. Is it Chloe, Paul, Appollos, Cephas; Luther, Calvin, Christ?

GROUP: Her sweet communion, solemn vows, her hymns of love and praise.

LEADER: I love institutional churches, sometimes under attack; sometimes assembling baskets for the needy, providing wedding receptions, preaching Christ.

GROUP: Jesus, Friend divine, our Savior and our King!

LEADER: I love problem churches: old as the New Testament and as new as the last church council meeting, seeking improvement but often failing.

GROUP: Thy hand, from every snare and foe, shall deliver'rance bring.

LEADER: I love Protestant suburban churches, somewhat sophisticated; well-organized, services and activities programmed to meet every need.

GROUP: Sure as your truth shall last, to Zion shall be given —

LEADER: I love all churches with endless "hypocrites" included, and all manner of faults, mistakes, yet ever heeding Christ in attempted mission.

GROUP: The brightest glories earth can yield and brighter bliss of heaven.

ALL: "And all that believed were together, and had all things in common." And the Lord added to the country church, city church, black church, Catholic church, mission church, house church, Quaker church, denominational church, institutional church, problem church, suburban church, all churches — those that are being saved. Amen.

— **Author unknown**

❊ The Greatest Power in the World
Meditation

World-wide Communion Sunday begins out in the Pacific Ocean, just west of the international date line. Christians under the palm trees of Fiji and Tonga are the first to receive the symbols of Christ's life and sacrifice. Then Christians in the Philippines, Japan, Hong Kong, Indonesia, and other lands of Eastern Asia share in the sacred service.

Follow the journey in your mind's eye, as Christians in Thailand, Burma, India, Ceylon, Pakistan, the Middle East, and Eastern Africa, worshiping in many and varied church structures, observe the Lord's Supper.

Europe, West Africa, Latin America, the churches of continental United States and Canada, and finally those of the fiftieth state, Hawaii, complete the universal observance of the central Christian act of worship.

No other symbolic act of Christians is so universal as the communion. Nearly every Christian group observes it. The particular forms of observance vary greatly, as do interpretations of its meaning. We bow in sorrow to think that some who call themselves Christian refuse to receive communion with certain other Christians. Yet in spite of this, the communion table remains a symbol of universal friendship. Breaking bread together is an act of community; sharing a cup is the sharing of life.

Imagine, if you will, a table so long it reaches around the globe. Around it gather all the Christians of the world. The appearance of the guests at this table varies greatly. At one end dark complexions predominate, at another light, because of geographical differences. Yet together they constitute one great family—with internal differences to be sure, as all families have, but acknowledging one God, one Lord and Savior.

The church does not begin and end on our own main street, nor on any other main street on our continent. It communes with its Lord in every land and in nearly every language. This is a thrilling fact that can come alive for all of us through Worldwide Communion Sunday.

A former outcaste in India trembled as he took the cup at the communion service. Afterwards he explained, "I felt that I had in my hand a power greater than any the world has ever known, a power to unite people everywhere in the bonds of community; a power far greater than the nuclear bomb, which can unite people only in complete and utter destruction." Power is released when a symbol like that is used around the world.

— **William Charles Walzer**[39]

The Mission of the Church

✳ The Meaning of Mission
Meditation

"Mission . . ." "Oh, yes," says someone, "foreign missions. The Chinese, you know. But, of course, all the missionaries were driven out of China, so there is no mission there any longer. A shame, isn't it, that missions failed so miserably. But, then, people seldom appreciate what you do for them. Well, our church won't have to send any more money over there now. I used to worry about doing that anyway. There are so many uses for it at home, you know."

"Mission . . ." "Why, our church supports one of those," says another. "That little hall down in the slum section. Drunks and bums come for coffee and doughnuts, and they have a religious service for them. It's nice to get them in off the street that way. Then, too, that little preacher down there—it's good to have places of that sort for people like him to work. He doesn't have much ability. No background, you know. He could never handle a church like ours."

"Mission . . ." "I remember when I was just a youngster, there was some sort of mission somewhere away off — Kentucky, maybe it was. I can't remember just where. Somewhere up in the mountains, in backwoods country. I recall so well my mother taking things over to the church to pack in a big barrel to send off to these folks. It was a lot of work, of course, but it was a good way to get our old things cleared out. They pile up so much if you don't go through them and discard some occasionally."

For most of us, descriptions like these express what the word mission means. We think of it as a branch of the church, an adjunct to the church, one activity in which the church is engaged, but something quite other than the church itself. We think that mission involves a task for a missionary society, or a few odd souls who go to the ends of the earth, or some second-rate people who cannot work well in what we think of as normal situations. But this is to misunderstand the nature of the church's mission.

Mission is not a special function of a part of the church. It is the whole church in action. It is the body of Christ expressing Christ's concern for the whole world. It is God's people seeking to make all persons members of the people of God. Mission is the function for which the church exists. "You are . . . God's own people," said Peter to the church. But why? For what purpose had God made them God's own? The answer is plain: *that you may declare the wonderful deeds of God who called you out of darkness into his marvelous light*" (1 Peter 2:9). To receive God's kindness in being made a member of God's people lays upon everyone the obligation to declare that kindness so that others, too, may become God's people. The church is *called out* of the world in order to *go to* the world. "They are not of the world," said Jesus, "even as I am *not of the world*. As thou didst send me *into the world*, so I have sent them *into the world*" (John 17:16, 18). It is the church's mission to be Christ's action in the world now.

— **Donald G. Miller**[40]

✳ **In Peace Let Us Pray**
Prayer

Russian Orthodox Christians pray this beautiful prayer every Sunday morning, indeed every time they gather to celebrate the liturgy. They have been doing so for nearly a thousand years! The deep concern for peace which it evidences is not new, but has been central in Christians' prayers and actions from the beginning. This ancient prayer illustrates that, for it has been part of the worship of all Eastern Orthodox Christians across the centuries. It is in fact the prayer which begins the Liturgy of St. John Chrysostom, which all of them use throughout the year.

This prayer could take on a very special significance during these days of tension and danger in the relations between the United States and the Soviet Union if Christians in both places pray the same prayer for peace as they gather to worship their common Lord. The prayer has been adapted for use in the United States by the Orthodox Church in America.

LEADER: In peace let us pray to the Lord.

PEOPLE: Lord have mercy.*

LEADER: For the peace from above, and for our salvation, let us pray to the Lord.

PEOPLE: Lord have mercy.

LEADER: For the peace of the whole world; for the welfare of the holy churches of God, and for the unity of all people, let us pray to the Lord.

PEOPLE: Lord have mercy.

LEADER: For this holy community of faith, and for those who with faith, reverence and love of God enter herein, let us pray to the Lord.

PEOPLE: Lord have mercy.

LEADER: For our pastor(s), for all clergy, for all who bear office in the church, for all of the people of God in all times and places, let us pray to the Lord.

PEOPLE: Lord have mercy.

LEADER: For the President of the United States of America and all civil authorities, for the leaders of all nations and for those who serve in the United Nations, let us pray to the Lord.

PEOPLE: Lord have mercy.

*The expression "Lord have mercy" (*Kyrie Eleison* in Greek) in this prayer is not necessarily a plea for forgiveness. It is instead a proclamation of one's faith in the presence and power of God.

LEADER: That God will aid them and grant them wisdom and strength to struggle for justice and peace.

PEOPLE: Lord have mercy.

LEADER: For this community, and for every city and land, and for the faithful who dwell in them, let us pray to the Lord.

PEOPLE: Lord have mercy.

LEADER: For healthful seasons, for abundance of the fruits of the earth and for peaceful times, let us pray to the Lord.

PEOPLE: Lord have mercy.

LEADER: For travelers by sea, by land and by air; for the sick and the suffering; for refugees and the homeless; for prisoners and their salvation; for the poor and the needy, let us pray to the Lord.

PEOPLE: Lord have mercy.

LEADER: For our deliverance from all tribulation, wrath, danger and necessity, let us pray to the Lord.

PEOPLE: Lord have mercy.

LEADER: Help us; save us; have mercy upon us and keep us, O God, by your grace.

PEOPLE: Lord have mercy.

LEADER: Calling to remembrance our mothers and fathers in the faith, with all of God's saints let us commend ourselves and each other, and all our life unto Christ our God.

PEOPLE: To you, O lord.

LEADER: O Lord our God, whose power is beyond anything that we can imagine, whose glory is greater than our ability to know, whose mercy knows no limits, and whose love toward humankind is deeper than our capacity to understand: Do, O Master, in your tender compassion look upon us and upon this holy community of faith and grant us and those who pray with us your rich blessings and benefits. For unto you are due all glory, honor and worship: to the Father, and to the Son, and to the Holy Spirit: now and ever and unto ages of ages.

ALL: Amen.[41]

✳ For Living Saints
Hymn

> For living saints who labor bravely on,
> Who keep the faith through battles lost or won,

To Christ their leader let our praise be sung.
Alleluia! Alleluia!

In days of joy, in suffering's darkest night,
Be thou, O Christ, their constant, shining light,
That none may falter in the fiercest fight.
Alleluia! Alleluia!

O may all Christians be as true and bold
As those who lived and died in days of old,
That in our time the Good News may be told.
Alleluia! Alleluia!

Bind all together in love's service strong,
Fighting for all 'gainst every human wrong,
That all may join in resurrection song.
Alleluia! Alleluia!

— **Herman F. Reissig**[42]

To be sung to R. Vaughan Williams' "Sine Nomine" ("For All the Saints Who From Their Labors Rest").

✳ Christ Has Called Us
Hymn

Christ has called us to new visions,
Here to celebrate and praise,
Here confess our old divisions,
Here our peace-petitions raise.
 Come repentant, come forgiving,
 Come in joy and hope and prayer,
 Christ, once crucified, now living,
 Bids us faith and love to share.
As we listen to each other,
As we speak in joy and pain,
We become as sister, brother,
Reconciled, at one again.
 Only thus in work and feeling
 For our neighbor far or near
 Can we worship God, revealing
 Gifts of grace among us here.

MEN: All creation struggles, yearning
For a time of true shalom.

■ 127 ■

WOMEN: Are we trying? Are we learning
Now to make the earth our home?

ALL: For the hungry and despairing,
For the poor of all the earth,
Make us partners, burdens sharing,
Bringing all a sense of worth.
Christ still calls us, young and aging,
Men and women, bound and free,
Colors, talents, thoughts engaging,
Joined in one community.
Christ remolding, healing, leading
Sins forgiven! Life restored!
Let us live, God's justice heeding,
Strengthened by our risen Lord.

— Jane Parker Huber[43]

To be sung to the tune "In Babilone" ("There's a Wideness in God's Mercy").

Personal Religious Living: Stewardship and Service

For the Christian, faith and religious practice eventually become intensely personal. Worship is not merely an abstract concept; it is more than a program to be relished or enjoyed. Worship eventually becomes life itself. The Christian experience thus becomes life changing. Some call this process being born again. Some speak of the sense of being called that they know in their choice of a vocation. This process does not happen in the same way to two persons, and it is therefore wrong for one person to expect anyone else to respond the same way that person does. It is right, however, for all Christians—perhaps especially for young Christians—to live expectantly, to be watchful and ready. For sometime, someplace, in some common place, the still small voice will come.

Worship is one place in which to be expectant. The resources in this section were chosen to help you open doors and windows. They are selected from a larger reservoir of written materials that suggest ways to respond to the gifts of the Creator. In the end these materials may be summarized by three words: worship, stewardship, and service.

✳ Scripture Readings

Who will go for us?—Isaiah 6:1–8
Let your light shine—Matthew 5:12–16
The good and faithful servant—Matthew 25:14–28
As you did it to one of the least—Matthew 25:35–40
If anyone serves me—John 12:24–26
Living the Christian life—Romans 12:1–11
God or Caesar—Mark 12:13–17

✳ Hymns

"Christ of the Upward Way"
"Light of the World, We Hail Thee"
"The Voice of God Is Calling"
"We Thank Thee, Lord"
"Lord, Speak to Me"
"Now in the Days of Youth"
"Take My Life and Let It Be"
"I Sing a Song of the Saints of God"
"God of Grace and God of Glory"

✳ Calls to Worship

And Christ said to them: "You shall be my witnesses in Jerusalem and
in all Judea and Samaria and to the end of the earth" (Acts 1:8b).

Holy, holy, holy is the Lord of hosts;
the whole earth is full of God's glory (Isa. 6:3b).

LEADER: Our help is in the name of the Lord.

GROUP: Who made heaven and earth.

LEADER: Praise the Lord!

GROUP: The Lord's name be praised!

LEADER: O God, open us to the powerful winds of your Spirit.

PEOPLE: Open our eyes to the wonders of your creation.

LEADER: Open our nostrils to the smells of life.

PEOPLE: Open our ears to words of justice and truth.

LEADER: Open our mouths to the taste of freedom and love.

PEOPLE: Open our arms to the touch of our sisters and brothers.

— J.M.B.

✻ Gracious God, You Have Given Us Much
Prayer

Gracious God, you have given us much.
> For this we are grateful.
> We humbly confess that we have not used your gifts wisely. We have wasted our time and our resources. We have wasted our money. We have hidden our abilities. For this we are truly sorry.
> Guide us so that from now on we may use your gifts wisely in the service of others. That is where we will find your kingdom. Amen.

— J.M.B.

✻ You Have Called Us Forth
Prayer

O God of Rachel, Leah, and Ruth;
God of Abraham, Isaac, and Jacob:
You have called us forth to a new land so many times—
> and you have watched us draw back into the safe ways of our homeland.

You have called us into new ways of being and doing
> and you have watched us cling to false securities,

You have called us to live life to the fullest—
> and you have watched us deny our own potential as ones created in your image.

And yet, O God, we come today in the belief that our fears can be overcome,
> and that we can learn to live boldly on the edge of life;
> that we, like Ruth, can follow to a new land, where you are our God.
> Amen.

— J.M.B.

✻ Then Only Shall I Dare
Reading

> Today I shall stretch forth my mind
> And it shall go
> Into the far-off, misty places of the earth.
> I shall walk beside the laborers in the rice fields
> Ankle-deep all day in mud;
> I shall beat clothing on flat rocks;
> I shall reach my hand into the ever-bubbling pot

and draw out whale meat.
Today I shall smell spicy bark,
And know the feel of ironwood and jade.

Today, I shall stretch forth my heart
And it shall feel
The terrors of the unlearned ones
Who live in constant fear of evil things.
And I shall hear the sick
Cry out as the witch doctor enters.
I shall know the thirst of the illiterate
Who long to read.
I shall see children sold as slaves,
And watch starved babies eating grass.

Today I shall stretch forth my hands
And I shall share
My bounty with the world's less fortunate;
I shall have a part in the teaching of the world,
And feeding of its poor,
The clothing of its naked shivering ones.
With my help shall its tortured flesh be healed;
Then—only then,
Can I endure my warmth and light and food.
Then only shall I dare to kneel and pray.

— **Margaret Chaplin Anderson**[44]

✳ I Will Go
Meditation in choric speech

DARK VOICES: When God began to create the heavens and the earth, the
earth was a desolate waste, with darkness covering the abyss and a
tempestuous wind raging over the surface of the waters.

LIGHT VOICES: Then God said, "Let there be light!" And there was light;
and God saw that the light was good.

UNISON: And God saw that the light was good.

LIGHT VOICES: God created human beings in God's own image; in the
image of God they were created; God saw that all that had been made
was very good.

SOLO 1: Generation upon generation see the light and the goodness of
    God,
    But the godly cease to be,

For the faithful disappear from the earth.
They speak lies each with a neighbor;
With false lip and double heart they speak.

SOLO 2: Woe to those who call evil good,
And good evil;
Who count darkness as light,
And light as darkness!

SOLO 3: The prophet sees visions and dreams dreams.
He sees the sin of his people, but all is not despair.
The people that walked in darkness
Have seen a great light;
Those who dwelt in a land of deep darkness—
On them has light shone.

SOLO 4: Upon whom has light shone?
And who makes the light to shine?

DARK VOICES: You are the light of the world! A city that is built upon a hill cannot be hidden. People do not light a lamp and put it under a peck-measure; they put it on its stand and it gives light to everyone in the house. Your light must burn in that way among the nations.

UNISON: Go to the whole world and proclaim the good news to all the creation.

SOLO 1: Then I heard the voice of the Lord saying, "Whom shall I send, and who will go for us?"

SOLO 2: Let me first go and bury my father.

SOLO 3: I cannot go, for I have my business to look after.

SOLO 4: I am not a leader.

SOLO 5: My mother is ill. I cannot leave her.

DARK VOICES: The curtains of the sanctuary were torn asunder, and a darkness fell upon the earth. And there was silence as of misery and death.

LIGHT VOICES: But out of the darkness there came a great light.

SOLO 1: I saw him die on the cross.

SOLO 2: He had a great love for everyone.

SOLO 3: That is why he gave his life for them.

SOLO 4: And for us.

SOLO 5: He said that whoever believed in him will do such things as he does, and things greater yet.

UNISON: The Spirit of the Lord God is upon me,
For the Lord has anointed me;
The Lord has sent me to bring good news to the lowly,
To bind up the brokenhearted,
To proclaim liberty to the captives,
And release to the prisoners;
To proclaim the year of the Lord's favor.

SOLO 1: Once again I hear the voice of the Lord saying, "Whom shall I send, and who will go for us?"

UNISON: Go to the whole world and proclaim the good news to all the creation.

SOLO 1: Then I heard the voice of the Lord saying, "Whom shall I send, and who will go for us?"

SOLO 2: I will go, for I must share my new happiness with others.

SOLO 3: I will go, to heal sick bodies and to work to restore life to the dying.

SOLO 4: I will give my money that others may go.

SOLO 5: I will go to bring the new light to others, for it is a great light that shines within me.

UNISON: The light is still shining in the darkness, for the darkness has never put it out. Your light can shine within you. Open your heart to love all creatures of every race and nation. Your hands can build peace and good will. Your lives can be given in service, here and in any land.

— Adapted by **Barbara Fuchs**[45]

✳ A Mail Carrier's Witness
Reading

He was a mail carrier and war was not his game. Yet during World War II he was sent from his home in a village at the foot of Mount Fuji to Guadalcanal, to fight with Japanese troops.

When Americans attacked, the Japanese were greatly outnumbered. In retreat, the mail carrier escaped to the jungle with a few of his friends. One by one, they succumbed to hunger and disease.

The last survivor, the young Japanese lay on the ground one day ill and starving. He heard the sound of footsteps approaching through the brush, and a moment later three armed soldiers stood over him. Too weak to raise his hands in surrender, he waited for the vicious thrust that would end his life.

One of the soldiers knelt beside him, and he heard an amazing word: "Friend." Strong arms lifted him, and he lost consciousness with the word "friend" still ringing in his ears.

Many days later he found himself in a hospital bed in New Zealand. He was a prisoner of war, but he was kindly treated, and a chaplain visited him every day. Before his release, he became a Christian.

After he returned home, he led his family to Christianity. When he acquired a house, he dedicated it with a candlelight service and made it available for the prayer meetings of his rural church. His daily witness has been best described by those who speak of him as "the mail carrier who delivers the gospel along with the mail."[46]

✳ Blest Be the Tie That Binds
A hymn meditation

Many hymns have been written at great moments in great lives. This is the story of one such hymn and of the dedicated man who wrote it.

John Fawcett was born in Yorkshire, England, in 1739. He was left an orphan at the age of twelve and was apprenticed to a tailor. In his apprenticeship, he had to work fourteen hours a day; but somehow with great persistence, he taught himself to read. At fifteen, inspired by a sermon, he decided to become a preacher.

John Fawcett's first parish, in Wainsgate, England, was a straggly cluster of houses with a small group of people who could neither read nor write. The parishioners were poor farmers and shepherds, but they had built a small, damp church with little stools instead of pews. As their minister, John Fawcett received only twenty pounds a year salary and with his wife boarded around at the homes in the parish. After their four children were born, the Fawcetts lived in such poverty that a typical day's meals consisted of porridge for breakfast, potatoes for dinner, and potatoes for supper.

At long last a call came from Carter's Lane Baptist Church in London. This meant a larger salary, a wider field of usefulness, and a chance for self-improvement. John and his wife decided to accept the call to the new church; but as they were leaving, the tears and devotion of the people at Wainsgate touched them deeply.

Then the heart had its way over the head. The Fawcetts stayed for a ministry of fifty-four years in Wainsgate and nearby Heben Bridge. The Sunday after he reached his decision Mr. Fawcett preached from the text in Luke 12:15: "One's life does not consist of the abundance of possessions." After the sermon, he lined out, and the congregation sang, the hymn he had written the previous midnight: "Blest Be the Tie That Binds."

This self-sacrificing decision on the part of John and Mary Fawcett brought a new impulse to the preacher's mind and a new power. He opened a training school for young preachers, published a volume of hymns, built a new meetinghouse, and wrote several books.

The hymn "Blest Be the Tie That Binds" is John Fawcett's monument. For nearly two hundred years it has been the parting benediction upon all kinds of religious gatherings the world around.

— B.J.B.

✳ A Life of Reconciliation
Meditation on 1 Peter 4:8

Each day, at the sixth hour—the hour of the crucifixion—the Orthodox churches in the Middle East relive the ultimate hour in which God's love for us was fully manifest on Calvary. The faithful pray:

O Christ, our God, who at this hour didst stretch out thy loving arms upon the cross that all might be gathered unto thee. . . .

This is the kind of love about which Peter writes in his epistle. It is the love that cancels sins and abolishes death. It is the love of God's suffering servant. According to the second century saint Ignatius of Antioch, it demonstrates the truth of Christ's humanity, which he calls a "mystery of shouting accomplished in the silence of God" [See Ephesians 19:1].

A young man wrote from the inferno of the shelling of Beirut to a friend living abroad:

Something has changed deep inside me. Every shell that falls in our area of town triggers a silent cry that tears me apart. Too many people have died. We carry our dead within us like scars. I have come to realize how essential it is for us, in the midst of this daily encounter with death, to let life reign on our faces. Only love can accomplish that sort of miracle in us. Without love you cannot share the burdens of those still living. For them you need that love which bears all things. Grounded in it you learn slowly that what is important is not to take a stand in one "camp" or the other. It is rather to love others for the truth that they are hoping. . . .

"Keep your love for one another at full strength for love cancels innumerable sins" [1 Peter 4:8 NEB]. You find that sooner or later, as you grow into this kind of bond, that you are unquestionably engaged. A newly-created human reality is laid in your arms. In a receptive hour of your life, you meet a person about whom there is something you cannot grasp in any objective way. It "says" something to you. It speaks something that enters your life. Perhaps it is something about the person; perhaps she needs you. Or it can be something about yourself.

A child has clutched your hand and you answer for its touch. Perhaps a host of people move about you and you answer for their need.

You cannot describe the person or persons through whom something has been said to you. But in each instance, a word requiring an answer has happened to you—an outstretched hand requiring your loving grasp. A word made face. A look made presence. And the silence of this presence speaks to you in the form of a mystery, a revelation which has become near, accessible to you.

Only after such experiences can we realize that as we wrestle together with our situation, in the light of what we know of God, that our knowledge is deepened and widened. When it is filled with human content, with the truth of Christ's humanity, life becomes a relationship to be received and experienced with gratitude and joy. Life becomes a process of mutual transformation in which the law of the point of view no longer rules. Life of this kind keeps love for one another at full strength.

— **Frieda Haddad**[47]

✳ **Who? Me?**
Prayer

>Me? On bended knees?
>Head bowed down
>in sorrow and silence?
>Listening with an inner ear
>for the voice of a spirit?
>Acknowledging a creator
>who permits my existence?
>Seeking guidance for my
>every thought and act?
>Me? Relinquishing my judgments,
>my rights, my opinions, my will?
>Yes. Me.
>Thank you, Lord, for choosing me.

— **Ruth Kaufmann**[48]

✳ **Revelations**
Poem

>We climb, we slip,
>we struggle, and fall,
>to find out in the end
>Jesus Christ is Lord of all.

— **Randy E. Dyer** [49]

✳ Benedictions

Go forth into the world in peace, to serve God with gladness.
Be of good courage; hold fast to that which is good;
> render to no one evil for evil;
> strengthen the fainthearted;
> support the afflicted;
> honor all people;
> love and serve God,
> rejoicing in the power of the Holy Spirit.

May the love of the Lord Jesus draw you to himself.
May the power of the Lord Jesus strengthen you in his service.
May the joy of the Lord Jesus fill your spirit.
And the blessing of God Almighty, the Creator, the Redeemer,
  and the Comforter,
be upon you and remain with you, forever. Amen.

✳ The Peace

LEADER: Lord Jesus Christ, you told your apostles:
"Peace I leave with you, my peace I give to you."
Look not on our sins but on the faith of your church.
In order that your will be done,
grant us always this peace, and guide us toward
the perfect unity of your kingdom, forever.

GROUP: Amen.

LEADER: The peace of the Lord be with you always.

GROUP: And also with you.

LEADER: Let us give one another a sign of reconciliation and peace.
(Each person is invited to greet those around, saying, for example, "Peace be with you.")

Creation and Ecology

We take great joy in God's creation. The sun and sand and surf of the seaside evoke not only recreational pleasure but wonder at the power of the Creator. Fields of newly sprouted corn or wheat ready for harvest are evidence of ways that God shares with men and women the creative power of helping to feed other people. But one only needs to see the eroded hillsides of land improperly farmed, or contemplate the acres of soil paved over to accommodate the armies of cars and trucks, or wipe away the tears that come with polluted air, to see how human beings have abused their environment.

With the psalmist we can "lift up our eyes to the hills" seeking the help that comes from God, for the out-of-doors evokes a sense of worship as little else does. For a worship setting in the open, no background other than the natural scene is necessary. Occasionally, at a campsite or church-owned recreation or retreat center, a stone altar and/or a rustic cross is already in place. When using a theme such as "Joy in God's Creation" indoors, mosses, stones, wild flowers, or leaves may be arranged on the worship table or altar. Reproductions of *St. Francis and the Birds* by Giotto or the *Birth of Adam* by Michelangelo would be appropriate, as would a map of the solar system.

Services for Creation

✳ Scripture Readings

> The story of creation — Genesis 1
> The heavens tell the glory of God — Psalm 19
> Worship the Lord in holy array — Psalm 96:6–13
> Thou didst set the earth on its foundations — Psalm 104
> The Lord is my shepherd — Psalm 23

✳ Hymns

> "All Beautiful the March of Days"
> "All Creatures of Our God and King"
> "Beauty Around Us"
> "Day Is Dying in the West" *(evening)*
> "For the Beauty of the Earth"
> "Fairest Lord Jesus"
> "God of the Earth and Sky and Sea"
> "God Who Touchest Earth With Beauty"
> "Now the Day Is Over" *(evening)*
> "When Morning Gilds the Skies" *(morning)*
> "The Sun Is on the Land and Sea" *(morning)*

✳ Calls to Worship at Any Hour

O come, let us worship and bow down,
  let us kneel before the Lord, our Maker!
For this is our God,
  and we are the people of God's pasture,
  and the sheep of God's hand (Ps. 95:6–7a).

The earth is the Lord's and the fullness thereof,
  the world and those who dwell therein;
for God has founded it upon the seas,
  and established it upon the rivers (Ps. 24:1–2).

✳ Call to Worship at Morning Services

This is the day which the Lord has made;
  let us rejoice and be glad in it (Ps. 118:24).

✳ Call to Worship at Evening Services

From the rising of the sun to its setting
the name of the Lord is to be praised! (Ps. 113:3).

✳ Thou Hast Lifted the Mountains
Prayer

God of universal matter, thou hast lifted the mountains out of the level
  of thy far-spread plains.
Thy hand has held them aloft through the silent nights, wreathed them
  in the mystery of clouds, touched them with the glory of the
  sunrise.
God of universal life, set thou a mountain in my mind.
Lift up within my heart, I pray thee, some mighty and selfless
  ambition.
Raise above the common level some cause to dominate me as this
  mountain does its world.
Grant me a vast purpose for which to live.
Hold it aloft within me through the dark and silent days of life.
Wreathe it in the mystery of undiscovered truth.
Touch it into glory with the sunrise of thy will.
Let it redeem the littleness of life by the touch of its greatness.
Set thou a mountain in my mind. Amen.

— **Percy R. Hayward**[50]

✳ We Thank Thee for This Universe
Prayer

O God, we thank thee for this universe, our great home; for its vastness and its riches, for the manifoldness of the life which teems upon it and of which we are a part. We praise thee for the arching sky and the blessed winds, for the driving clouds and the constellations on high. We praise thee for the salt sea and the running water, for the everlasting hills, for the trees, and for the grass under our feet. We thank thee for our senses by which we can see the splendor of the morning, and hear the jubilant songs of love, and smell the breath of the springtime. Grant us, we pray thee, a heart wide open to all this joy and beauty, and save our souls from being so steeped in care or so darkened by passion that we pass heedless and unseeing when even the thornbush by the wayside is aflame with the glory of God. Amen.

— **Walter Rauschenbusch**[51]

✳ Canticle of the Sun
Prayer

O most high, almighty, good Lord God, to thee belong praise, glory, honor, and all blessing.

Praised be my Lord God with all creatures and especially our brother the sun, who brings us the day and the light; fair is he and shines with a very great splendor: O Lord, he signifies to us thee.

Praised be my Lord for our sister the moon, and for the stars, the which he hath set clear and lovely in the heavens.

Praised be my Lord for our brother the wind, and for the air and cloud, calms and all weather by the which thou upholdest life in all creatures.

Praised be the Lord for our sister water, who is very serviceable unto us and humble and precious and clean.

Praised be my Lord for our brother fire, through which thou givest us light in the darkness; and he is bright and pleasant and very mighty and strong.

Praised be my Lord for our mother the earth, the which doth sustain us and keep us, and bringeth forth divers fruits and flowers of many colors, and grass.

Praised be my Lord for all those who pardon one another for love's sake, and who endure weakness and tribulation; blessed are they who peaceably shall endure, for thou, O Most High, shalt give them a crown.

Praise ye and bless the Lord and give thanks unto God and serve
God with great humility.

— **Francis of Assisi**[52]

✳ For the Beauty of Earth and Sea
Prayer

> We give you thanks, most gracious God.
> for the beauty of earth and sea;
> for the richness of mountains, plains, and rivers;
> for the songs of birds and the loveliness of flowers.
> We praise you for these good gifts,
> and pray that we may safeguard them for our posterity.
> Grant that we may grow in our grateful enjoyment
> of your abundant creation;
> to the honor and glory of your Name, now and for ever.
>   Amen.[53]

✳ Prayer at Morning Services

Creator Spirit, who broodest everlastingly over the lands and waters of
earth, enduing them with forms and colors which no human skill can
copy, give me today, I beseech thee, the mind and heart to rejoice in
thy creation.

Forbid that the lure of the market place should ever entirely steal
my heart away from the love of the open acres and the green trees;

Forbid that under the low roof of workshop or office or study I
should ever forget thy great overarching sky;

Forbid that when all thy creatures are greeting the morning with
songs and shouts of joy, I alone should wear a dull and sullen face;

Let the energy and vigor which in thy wisdom thou hast infused
into every living thing stir today within my being, that I may not be
among thy creatures as a sluggard and a drone;

And above all, give me grace to use these beauties of earth [around]
me and this eager stirring of life within me as a means whereby my
soul may rise from creature to Creator, and from nature to nature's
God. Amen.

—**John Baillie**[54]

✳ Prayer at Evening Services

O thou Creator of all things that are, I lift up my heart in gratitude to
thee for this day's happiness: for the mere joy of living; for all the

sights and sounds around me; for the sweet peace of the country and the pleasant bustle of the town; for all things bright and beautiful and gay; for friendship and good company; for work to perform and the skill and strength to perform it; for a time to play when the day's work was done, and for health and a glad heart to enjoy it.

— **John Baillie**[55]

✳ A Statement of Faith

LEADER: Some thousands of millions of years ago

GROUP: We believe in God:

LEADER: a fragment of matter composed of particularly stable atoms

GROUP: who calls

LEADER: was detached from the surface of the sun

GROUP: the worlds

LEADER: This fragment began to condense, to roll itself up, to take shape.

GROUP: into being,

LEADER: The curve doubles back, the surface contracts; the solid disintegrates, the liquid boils, the germ cell divides, intuition suddenly bursts.

GROUP: creates us and sets before us the ways

LEADER: We are responsible for the quality of our future. We are evolving into an interdependent whole of which every person is called upon to become a vital part.

GROUP: of life

LEADER: Every organization insensitive to our need for personal involvement in the well-being of our fellow humans is disintegrating

GROUP: and death.

LEADER: Shock troopers of evolutionary change are now attacking all separatist structures

GROUP: who judges people and nations:

LEADER: which are unresponsive to the need to participate responsibly in the improvement of human life. The power of the Incarnate Word penetrates matter itself.

GROUP: In Jesus Christ

LEADER: It descends into the deepest depths of the interior forces.

GROUP: God has come to us,

LEADER: In a spiritually converging world this "Christic" energy acquires an urgency and intensity.

GROUP: conquering sin and death and reconciling the world.

LEADER: God . . . is not withdrawn from us beyond the tangible sphere.

GROUP: God bestows upon us

LEADER: God is waiting for us at every moment in our action.

GROUP: the Holy Spirit

LEADER: Try with God's help

GROUP: and calls us into the church

LEADER: to perceive the connection . . . which binds your labor with the building of the Kingdom.

GROUP: to accept the cost and joy of discipleship

LEADER: Whoever has discovered . . . the secret of serving the evolving Universe and identifying with it

GROUP: to be servants in the service of the whole human family.

LEADER: for that one, shadows will disappear.

GROUP: God promises to all who trust in the gospel, forgiveness of sins and fullness of grace; courage in the struggle for justice and peace, the presence of the Holy Spirit in trial and rejoicing, and eternal life in that kingdom which has no end. Blessing and honor, glory and power be unto God. Amen.
— **Pierre Teilhard de Chardin and the United Church of Christ**[56]

✳ **How Can You Sell the Sky?**
Meditation

During the Indian Council in the Valley of Walla Walla in 1855, the whites proposed a treaty that would place three tribes on three reservations. Young Chief of the Cayuses opposed the treaty on the ground that Indians cannot sell, or buy, or give away land given them by the Great Spirit. In his speech Young Chief expressed from his depths the sense of the Indian relationship to the land. When asked to sell land to the whites, he said,

"I wonder if the ground has anything to say? I wonder if the ground is listening to what is said? I wonder if the ground would come alive and what is on it? I hear what the ground says. The ground says, 'It is the Great Spirit that placed me here. The Great Spirit tells me to take care of the Indians, to feed them aright. The Great Spirit appointed the roots to feed the Indians on. The water says the same thing. The Great Spirit directs me, Feed the Indians well. The grass says . . . Feed the Indians well.' "

Is it possible to view the land without some inner belief or faith about what it means? Our beliefs about the land may permit or even drive us to exploit, pollute and destroy. Or they may require us to love and care for it.

Rolling Thunder, a contemporary Shoshone Medicine Man, provided this evocative metaphor, "When you have pollution in one place it spreads all over. . . . The earth is sick now because the earth is being mistreated, and some of the problems that may occur, some of the natural disasters that might happen in the near future, are only the natural adjustments that have to take place to throw off sickness.

"A lot of things are on this land that don't belong there. They're foreign objects like viruses or germs. Now, we may not recognize the fact when it happens, but a lot of the things that are going to happen in the future will really be the earth's attempt to throw off some of these sicknesses. This is really going to be like fever or vomiting, what you might call physiological adjustment."

Chief Seattle's classic utterance sums it up:

"How can you buy or sell the sky, the warmth of the land? The idea is strange to us.

"If we do not own the freshness of the air and the sparkle of the water, how can you buy them?

"Every part of this earth is sacred to my people. Every shining pine needle, every sandy shore, every mist in the dark woods, every clearing and humming insect is holy in the memory of my people. The sap which courses through the trees carries the memory of the red man."

It may be tempting in this technological and urbanized world to discount the native American Indian way as sentimental, as naive, as primitive religion. But the issues today clamor for us to pay attention to the land. They are ecological—have we transgressed beyond the boundary of recovery from pollution, taken too many non-renewable resources, and over-used the land? They are political as different peoples and nations claim through religion, history and culture the same land. They are spiritual, with individuals feeling lost, without rootage, with no place to call home. However we conceptualize it, land is central to the present human struggles.

— **Norman W. Jackson**[57]

✶ Color in God's Creation
Meditation

We who are able to see color clearly in the world around us have no idea what it is to live without it. Even those who are color-blind to some degree are able to make out some colors, and it is rare indeed to find a person who sees only grays and blacks. Yet there are people who have been blind from birth who may never have perceived color or known the richness that it can add to life. Perhaps we can better appreciate color if we listen to a description of Helen Keller's ideas about color. This is taken from a preface to one of Helen Keller's books, and is written by Nella Braddy.

(Here the leader may wish to ask the group to listen to this quotation, first with their eyes closed, and then with their eyes open, looking at the color they find about them in nature.)

It is annoying to a certain type of mind to have Miss Keller describe something she obviously cannot know through direct sensation. The annoyance is mutual. These sensations, whatever expert opinion on them may be, are as real to her as any others. Her idea of color, to take only one instance, is built up through association and analogy. Pink is "like a baby's cheek or a soft Southern breeze." Gray is "like a soft shawl around the shoulders." Yellow is "like the sun. It means life and is rich in promise." There are two kinds of brown. One is "warm and friendly like leaf mold." The other is "like the trunks of aged trees with worm holes in them, or like withered hands." Lilac, which is her teacher's favorite color, "makes her think of faces she has loved and kissed." The warm sun brings out odors that make her think of red. Coolness brings out odors that make her think of green. A sparkling color brings to mind soap bubbles quivering under her hand.

— **Nella Braddy**[58]

A Liturgy for the Earth

Appropriate hymns could be sung just before Part I and Part II. In the litany in Part I the spoken phrase "Lord have mercy" could be replaced by the Kyrie on page 191.

✶ Call to Prayer

> O Great Spirit,
> Whose breath gives life to the world
> and whose voice is heard in the soft breeze,
> we need your strength and wisdom.

May we walk in Beauty. May our eyes
 ever behold the red and purple sunset.
Make us wise so that we may understand
 what you have taught us.
Help us learn the lessons you have hidden
 in every leaf and rock.
Make us always ready to come to you
 with clean hands and straight eyes
So when life fades, as the fading sunset,
 our spirits may come to you without shame.

— **From a Native American prayer**

LEADER: The earth is the Lord's and the fullness thereof,

ALL: The world and all those who dwell in it.

✳ Part I: The Sorrow of the Earth: Litany of Prayer

LEADER: The litany we will now use draws upon the symbolism of the
 American Indian people. Because the earth is the source of
 blessings — food, clothing, shelter, the seasons, healing
 medicines, beauty — and is the nurturer of life, the earth is
 personified in myth and poetry and called "mother." God, the
 creator and source of all life, is called Great Spirit. Mother
 Earth speaks:

VOICE: Listen, my children. The Spirit who moved over the dry land
 is not pleased. I am thirsty. Are you listening?

ALL: We are listening, Mother Earth. Speak.

VOICE: The Spirit who filled the waters is not pleased. I choke with
 debris and pollution. Are you listening?

ALL: We are listening. Mother Earth. Speak.

VOICE: The Spirit who brought beauty to the earth is not pleased. The
 earth grows ugly with misuse. Are you listening?

ALL: We are listening, Mother Earth. Speak.

VOICE: The Spirit who brought forth all the creatures of this earth is
 not pleased. My creatures are being destroyed. Are you
 listening?

ALL: We are listening, Mother Earth. Speak.

VOICE: The Spirit who gave humans life and a path to walk together
 is not pleased. You are losing your humanity and your
 footsteps stray from the path. Are you listening?

ALL: We are listening, Mother Earth.

LEADER: Let us pray. O God, you created the earth in goodness and in beauty. Forgive all that we have done to harm the earth.

PEOPLE: Lord have mercy.

LEADER: O God, you have filled the earth with food for our sustenance. Forgive us for not sharing the gifts of the earth.

ALL: Christ, have mercy.

LEADER: You have created us, O God, of one blood throughout the earth. Forgive us for not living as sisters and brothers should.

ALL: Lord, have mercy.

— **Sister Mary Rosita Shiosee, S.B.S.**

✳ Part II: The Healing of Earth's Wounds: Litany of Prayer

LEADER: Great Spirit, whose dry lands thirst, help us to find the way to refresh your lands.

ALL: We pray for your power to refresh your lands.

LEADER: Great Spirit, whose waters are choked with debris and pollution, help us to find the way to cleanse your waters.

ALL: We pray for your knowledge to find the way to cleanse the waters.

LEADER: Great Spirit, whose beautiful earth grows ugly with misuse, help us to find the way to restore the beauty of your handiwork.

ALL: We pray for your strength to restore the beauty of your handiwork.

LEADER: Great Spirit, whose creatures are being destroyed, help us to find the way to replenish them.

ALL: We pray for your power to replenish the earth.

LEADER: Great Spirit, whose gifts to us are being lost in selfishness and corruption, help us to find the way to restore our humanity.

ALL: We pray for your wisdom to find the way to restore our humanity.

✳ Silent Reflection

✳ Collective Prayer

ALL: Great Spirit, give us hearts to understand; never to take from creation's beauty more than we give; never to destroy wantonly for the furtherance of greed; never to deny to give our hands for the building of earth's beauty; never to take from her what we cannot use. Give us hearts to understand that to destroy earth's music is to create confusion; that to wreck her appearance is to blind us to beauty; that to callously pollute her fragrance is to make a house of stench; that as we care for her she will care for us. Amen.

✳ Dismissal

ALL: Now Talking God,
  With your feet I walk,
  I walk with your limbs,
  I carry forth your body,
  For me your mind thinks,
  Your voice speaks for me.
  Beauty is before me
  And beauty behind me.

Above and below me hovers the beautiful,
I am surrounded by it,
I am immersed in it.
In my youth I am aware of it,
And in old age
I shall walk quietly
The beautiful trail.[59]

(All walk out in silence.)

Jesus

"O come, let us adore him," we sing at Christmas time. The spiritual prompts us to yearn: "Lord I want to be like Jesus." And at Easter we proclaim, "Christ is risen! Indeed he is risen!"

So we seek not only to learn about and from Jesus but to worship him as the One who has helped us know God, the One whose face is the face of God. The materials in this section are designed to do both — to help us to know God as we know Jesus, and to worship them together.

The materials may be especially useful during Advent and Lent, times when attention is especially paid to Jesus. Many other materials may be found. For example, look through your hymnal to find those prayer hymns that are addressed to Christ. Then weave your worship service together, looking always to Jesus, "the pioneer and perfecter" of the faith.

✳ Call to Worship

LEADER: Come from the east and the west,
  from the north and the south,
  and worship the God of our mothers and our fathers;

the God of Jesus the Christ.
Christ is with you!

PEOPLE: And also with you.

LEADER: Christ is with us.

PEOPLE: Christ is in our midst.

LEADER: Let us pray:

ALL: Gracious God
gentle in your power
and strong in your tenderness,
You have brought us forth
from the womb of your being
and breathed into us the breath of life.
We know that we do not live by bread alone,
but by every word that comes from you.
Feed our deep hungers with the living bread
that you give us in Jesus Christ.
May his promise,
"Where two or three are gathered together in my name
there am I in the midst of them"
be fulfilled in us.
Make us a joyful company of your people
that with the faithful in every place and time
we may praise and honor you, God most high. Amen.

— J.M.B.

❊ Call to Worship

LEADER I: In the beginning was the Word.
The Word was with God
and the Word was God.

LEADER II: All that came to be has life in the Word
And that life is the light of the world.

LEADER I: The Word is the true light that enlightens all people.

LEADER II: He came into the world and the Word was made flesh.
To all who accept Christ and believe in his name,
he gives the power to become children of God.

LEADER I: He lives among us! And we see his glory!

LEADER II: The glory that is his as the only Son, full of grace and truth.

PEOPLE: Together, in joy, we adore thee, O God of love, O God of life.

— J.M.B.

✳ What Are You Saying to Us, Lord?
Reading in the form of a prayer

What are you saying to us, Lord?
We know that you spoke to prophets and holy ones of old.
You spoke to Jesus and we remember what he said to us.
By your Spirit you spoke to Matthew and Mark and Paul and the
    others.
And we know what your Spirit said to the saints and monks and
    reformers.
We know things you uttered through poets and painters and architects
    and composers.

But what are you saying to us now, Lord?
Could you raise your voice—or lower it?
Could you speak to us in events without ambiguity?
Speak to all of us—loud and clear, so that all of us together might say,
"This is what God wants; we will do what God wants."

We know, Lord, that the world is changing.
Things we thought were nailed down seem to be coming loose.
And the hopes we had for the future suddenly seem to be out of focus.
What is it that you are saying to us in all this?

Is it that justice and mercy and humility are still required of us if there
    is to be peace on earth?
Is it that those of us who think we are powerful are flawed by weakness
    and those who are powerless and oppressed are powerful because
    you are on their side?
Are you saying to us that we must still lose our lives for your sake in
    order to find them; that our souls shall find no rest until they rest
    in you?

But these things we have heard before, Lord.
Show us a sign and we will believe.

God says: You talk to me as if you were my equal . . . as if I were, like
    you, a human being.
Have you forgotten that I created the universe and yet creation does not
    embrace all of me?
My thoughts are not your thoughts and my ways are not your ways.
And I have given you a sign: my son, Jesus, crucified and raised from

the dead. In him and his life for others you can hear and see what
I am saying to you, even today.
Amen, Lord. Amen.

— **Robert V. Moss, Jr.**[60]

✳ **He Came Himself**
Poem

> He did not send technical assistance
> To our backward world;
> Gabriel and a company of experts
> With their know-how.
> He did not negotiate
> For the export of surplus grace
> On a long term loan.
> He did not arrange to send us food
> Or the cast-off garments of angels,
> Instead, He came Himself.
> He hungered in the wilderness,
> He was stripped naked on the cross,
> But hungering with us
> He became our bread,
> And suffering for us
> He became our joy.

— **Edith Lovejoy Pierce** [61]

✳ **Christ Is Present in the Hungry Poor**
Meditation on the biblical understanding of justice

"When I touch the body of the poor, I touch the body of Christ."
Mother Teresa of Calcutta said that. She also believes it! It is a
theological statement inviting assent from believers throughout the
world. When that worldwide assent of faith comes, the problem of
hunger will be no more!

Regrettably, however, most of the world's Christians see hunger as a
secular problem only. They fail to see, with the eye of faith, Christ
present and suffering in the hungry poor.

They recognize the importance of charity. And it is somehow
etched in their minds that "charity begins at home." But they do not
understand Dom Helder Camara, the archbishop of Recife, Brazil,
when he says that "the great charity of our time consists in helping
promote justice." For most Christians, hunger is a "charity" issue, not a
question of justice.

■ 151 ■

Emergency food assistance, relief shipments and similar donations are critically important in times of famine, flood, earthquake and similar disasters. But the deeper problem of chronic hunger which reduced the life chances of millions — probably five hundred million suffering people in the world today — is not touched by emergency relief efforts.

The Old Testament presents care for the poor and oppressed in terms of justice. In Isaiah 58:1–10, the prophet is to "declare to my people their transgressions," for "they ask me for righteous judgments. . . . Behold, in the day of your fast you . . . oppress all your workers. . . . Is not this the fast I choose . . . to let the oppressed go free and to break every yoke? Is it not to share your bread with the hungry?"

The Old Testament writers did not speculate about the nature of justice. They recorded concrete instances of justice and injustice in the lives of people. Modern scholarship locates justice as a central theme of Scripture but recognizes its relatedness to other themes like truth, loving mercy and fidelity to the covenant.

The just person of the Old Testament is depicted often in the Psalms, in Proverbs and the book of Job. In the Psalms we see that Yahweh rewards according to justice (18:20). The justice of the individual is depicted in Psalm 112. In Proverbs and Job the just one is a good steward of land and work animals (Job 31:13) and particularly one who cares for the poor, the fatherless, and the widow (Proverbs 29:7; Job 29:12–15).

In the New Testament, the main point to note about justice is its personification in Jesus Christ, "the just one" (Acts 3:14; 7:52). The works of Jesus are seen as works of justice (Mt. 18:23–24). Particular attention is to be paid to Matthew's last judgment scene, in that the "unjust" are condemned not because they failed to do what justice demanded, but because they did not know to whom they should do the works of justice, namely to the marginals and oppressed of society, to the hungry and those in prison. In the New Testament as the Old, caring for the marginals of society is a matter of justice.

In both his Gospel and Acts, Luke intended to present to early Christians a paradigm for living in their everyday environments. Of all the evangelists, Luke has Jesus sounding most like an Old Testament prophet in his condemnation of the rich (Luke 6:20) and wealth itself (12:16; 14:33). In fact, Luke is seen as the evangelist most interested in what today is called "social justice."

In *The Faith That Does Justice*, John R. Donahue points out that in Luke "the cause of the poor, the hungry and the oppressed is the cause of Jesus. He is the Son of Man, present in the least of his brothers and sisters. Christians are called on to bear one another's burdens. This is to fulfill the law of Christ, to be a just people. Engagement in the quest for justice is no more 'secular' than the engagement of Yahweh in the history of his people or the incarnation of Jesus into the world of human suffering. The Bible gives a mandate and a testament to Christians that, in their quest for justice, they are recovering the roots of the biblical tradition and are seeking to create the dwelling place for the word of God in human history."

Discussion, prayer, reflection and theological development along these lines must happen in the contemporary Christian community if hunger is to be overcome. We have a mandate, nothing less, than to eliminate this scourge from the face of the earth.

— **Edward J. Brady, S.J.**[62]

Jesus' Life Through Interpretations of Paintings

Each of the five meditations that follow is based on a well-known paint-ing of Jesus. We do not know, of course, what Jesus looked like. In each generation, and among many different ethnic groups, artists have sought to interpret the meaning of Jesus' life and ministry. If we look at the paintings in that context, each of them helps us to see another aspect of the one who means so very much to many different people. Each artist, therefore, is a witness — a "preacher" as it were — seeking to make Christ known.

The paintings chosen for these meditations are only representative of many that could have been used. They were selected because they are generally available, either as reproductions of the paintings or as slides that can be projected. Your church may have framed reproductions of some or all of them. Slides are usually available through resource cen-ters, religious bookstores or audiovisual libraries.

The meditations printed here could be used as part of a Lenten series on the Life of Christ. You might wish to broaden the selection by seeking contemporary or local interpretations as well as those from Africa or Asia. From a very different cultural background, you might wish to base an interpretation on an icon from the Orthodox tradition.

With each of the meditations based on paintings there are suggested biblical references and an appropriate hymn. Helpful material for inter-pretations of other art works may be found in a number of books, especially *The Gospel in Art* by Albert Edward Bailey.[63]

✳ **Jesus Calls Us**
Meditation inspired by Ernst Zimmerman's Christ and the Fishermen

This painting is based on Matthew 4:18–22. Appropriate hymns would include "Shepherd of Eager Youth," "Jesus Calls Us o'er the Tumult," and "Christ of the Upward Way." The second verse of "Dear Lord and Father" could be used as a response to prayer. (The first verse is difficult because it was written before sensitivity to inclusive language.)

* * *

In this picture Ernst Zimmerman, a German painter, helps us to see in our mind's eye something of the scene as it must have been on that long-ago day when Jesus called James and John, who were sons of a man named Zebedee. Zebedee was a fisherman, and his sons were following their father's calling.

Countless young people in all the long centuries since this meeting of Jesus with the sons of Zebedee have heard Christ's call. Some have gone at once. Some have worried and suffered because they could not "immediately leave their boats and their parents and follow him."

This painting shows us two determined young men. They were convinced. They knew their minds. The Master's call seemed clear enough — so clear that even as common fishermen they were able to understand it unmistakably.

They understood when he invited them to be his disciples and to be fishers of men and women. But their father was depending on their help with his fishing business.

"I, too, am depending on you," Jesus might have said.

And the young men must have pleaded with him, "Then come, talk with Zebedee our father." They went and found him working on the nets, carefully checking and mending them.

Zimmerman paints the face of the old man as that of one who finds it hard to understand the new approach to life that Jesus was recommending. He had been trained in the faith of his parents, and of their ancestors before them.

We see no impatience on Jesus' face. There is no hint of any sly wink from him to young John that would have said, "He's old and set in his ways. He'll never understand." No, that was not Jesus' way. The artist portrays Jesus deep in conversation with the old man, carefully explaining to him what he believes and what he wants James and John to do.

Look for a moment at the figure of Jesus. Note how earnestly he is speaking; how certain he is that he is speaking ultimate truth; how tenderly he touches Zebedee's wrist; how intimately they talk, almost as though they are completely unaware that the boys are right there listening to every word.

We might wonder whether Jesus succeeded in convincing Zebedee, if we hadn't already read the end of the story. "They left their boat and their father and followed him." These two determined boys were later called "sons of thunder," because they were so sure of what they believed.

— B.J.B. and J.M.B.

✳ Do We Mock Christ?
Meditation inspired by George Rouault's Christ Mocked by Soldiers

This painting is based on Matthew 27:27–31. Appropriate hymns would be "O Sacred Head, Now Wounded," "In the Hour of Trial," "When I Survey the Wondrous Cross," and other crucifixion hymns. The third verse of "Before the Cross of Jesus" is useful as a prayer response.

* * *

Many people do not care for Rouault's picture *Christ Mocked by Soldiers.* "It is entirely too modern," some say. "This isn't my Christ," others add.

This is precisely the reason for choosing this picture for a Lenten meditation. Lent reminds us that life has its times of difficulty and despair, and that Christ was called upon to endure the worst that people would inflict upon one another. This painting conveys, even shouts, the suffering of Jesus. Beside it even some crucifixion scenes in religious paintings appear placid.

Let us study the picture silently for a few moments, looking at the expressions on the faces . . . *(pause)* the effect of the bright colors . . . *(pause)* the eyes of Christ . . . *(pause).*

This is the moment before the soldiers laughed at Christ. The robe of regal red thrown over his naked shoulders anticipates their mockery.

Even though sorrow is plainly visible on his forehead, and even though his shoulders are weighted down by disappointment and apparent failure, the lines of Christ's body exhibit strength. His arms, lying as though shackled along his legs, are strong enough to have hefted a hammer — or brought healing to the sick. Though these arms be nailed to a cross in death, Christ will yet spread them wide in new life to welcome all of us to himself.

In this picture the soldiers stand at either side as though to prevent any escape through the door at the rear. Yet even between two guards it is the Christ, full-drawn, who is central. The heavy black lines and the bright colors, giving an effect of stained glass, leave little doubt as to who dominates the scene.

This is not to say that there is no anguish, no pain, no grief expressed in the picture. The eyes that saw a vision of a better world are closed. The lips that taught the love of God are silent before the malice of humanity. Here is the man of sorrows, acquainted with grief.

But the final mocking is not at the hands of the soldiers; it is in the brush of the artist. Known for his clowns and grotesque circus figures, Rouault has made the soldiers a part of his "clownerie." The soldiers seem dwarfed by the seated Christ. Their faces are smeared with grease paint and accented by puttied noses. The soldier on the left wears a silly blue hat. They that mock the Christ are but a fleeting and ineffective part of life. They are mocked by an eternal contemplation, sorrowful yet knowing that the world has been overcome.

— B.J.B. and J.M.B.

✳ Were You There?

Meditation based on El Greco's Crucifixion Over Toledo

This painting is based on Luke 23:44–49. Appropriate hymns include "Beneath the Cross of Jesus," "There Is a Green Hill Far Away," "In the Cross of Christ I Glory," and other crucifixion hymns. The spiritual "Were You There?" can be used as a prayer response, with verses alternated with prayers as in a litany.

* * *

In the sixteenth century, when El Greco was living in the monastery city of Toledo, Spain, it was customary for artists to honor their patrons by putting their portraits into religious pictures. In 1590, when El Greco painted a picture of Christ on the cross, he pictured in the foreground, not Jesus' disciples, but the men who had commissioned him to paint the picture.

It seems natural then that this artist should later paint a crucifixion scene over the skyline of the town he knew so well, for he had lived in Toledo for many years, and his paintings hung in the cathedral and many of the churches of the town.

El Greco's painting *Crucifixion Over Toledo* has a timeless, universal quality about it. Far more than those of his paintings that included pictures of his patrons, who often had more money than devotion, this picture gives one the feeling that it might be a picture of anywhere, or indeed everywhere.

Golgotha, the site of the actual crucifixion, was located on the edge of Jerusalem. The Golgotha pictured in the painting could be located on the outskirts of our town or any town. The buildings that loom behind the cross could be taken for the skyline of New York City, with the United Nations headquarters in the foreground and the television antennae atop the Empire State Building piercing the storm clouds. They could even be the outline of our own familiar city hall, the windows of our own school, the bell tower of our own church. The soldiers returning from their bloody work could be returning to our own town.

With his brushes and pigments El Greco asks for all time the question expressed so hauntingly in the spiritual "Were you there when they crucified my Lord?"

— B.J.B. and J.M.B.

✳ Is It I, Lord?

Meditation inspired by Leonardo da Vinci's The Last Supper

This painting is based on Mark 14:12–25. Appropriate hymns would be "Bread of the World, in Mercy Broken," "Lord, Enthroned in Heavenly Splendor," "Let Us Break Bread Together," "Here, O My Lord, I See Thee

Face to Face," and other communion hymns. For a response to prayer, the hymn "Be Known to Us in Breaking Bread" may be used.

* * *

In his painting *The Last Supper* Leonardo da Vinci has chosen to depict the moment when Christ says, "Verily I say unto you that one of you shall betray me." These unexpected words have fallen upon the group like an electric shock; they have broken the company into four distinct groups.

On the extreme left are Bartholomew, James the Less, and Andrew, all speechless and dumbfounded over the announcement. Bartholomew stares incredulously, Andrew protests by holding up both his hands, James cannot believe his ears and reaches over to Peter to verify the word. In the next group, Judas, smitten by his guilty conscience, recoils from the Master and instinctively clutches his bag that has been his undoing, while in his agitation he upsets the salt cellar. Peter leans forward with breathless haste and whispers, "Tell us who it is of whom he speaketh." John in utter distress sinks back toward Peter. On the extreme right, Simon holds out both hands as if to show his utter innocence of any treachery, while Thaddeus gazes earnestly into his face as much as to say, "This is preposterous! He is certainly mistaken"; and Matthew says excitedly, "But he says it is one of us!" — pointing the while toward Jesus with both his hands. In the right center is the most vigorous and interesting group. Each one is bidding for the Master's attention and expressing his unmistakable protest. Emotional and self-distrustful Thomas, with finger raised almost in the face of Jesus, exclaims, "Is it I, Lord?" James, acting surely his part as a "son of thunder," explodes with a double gesture of horror; and Philip pours out his soul in a look of utter sincerity while his hands would lay open his naked heart for inspection.[64]

With all these varied responses to Christ's announcement of his impending betrayal, surely one of them fits each of us. Think for a moment. Are you like Andrew, protesting that you would never betray Christ; or are you Simon, wearing an expression of utter innocence; or James, the son of thunder, exploding in horror?

If we would be true to ourselves, must we not at least ask Thomas' question, "Is it I, Lord?" And if we continue then to be true to our real selves, we may feel a little sneaking doubt rising within us. We will realize that we betray him, not for money necessarily, but in our own selfish interest, whenever we fail to put him first in our lives.

There are times when, smitten by a guilty conscience, we must ask Judas' question, "Is it I, Lord?" expecting Christ to answer, "Yes."

As they were eating, Jesus took bread, and blessed, and broke it, and gave it to the disciples and said, "Take, eat; this is my body." And he took a cup and when he had given thanks he gave it to them, saying, "Drink of it, all of you; for this is my blood of the covenant, which is poured out for many for the forgiveness of sins."

Though we come to Christ, knowing ourselves to be betrayers, we know, too, in his mercy that he forgives us and gives us the bread of life.

—B.J.B. and J.M.B.

✳ Do We Know Him?
Meditation inspired by Rembrandt's The Supper at Emmaus.

This painting is based on Luke 24:13–35. Appropriate hymns include "Be Known to Us in Breaking Bread," "Here, O My Lord, I See Thee Face to Face," "Come Ye Faithful, Raise the Strain," "The Day of Resurrection," and other Easter hymns. The first verse of "Break Thou the Bread of Life" may be used as a prayer response.

* * *

The day is far spent; the disciples, loath to part with the stranger whose insight is opening to them a new heaven and a new earth, have persuaded him to be their guest . . . at the simple evening meal. . . . The light falls golden from the window, illuminating vaguely the simple lines of the room. . . . It touches into life the raised hands of the younger man, the earnest face of the servant, Cleopas, thoughtful and fascinated; and then, reinforced by the reflection from the white cloth, it throws the central figure into strong relief against the dim wall. That face, etched by the brilliant light, is one of Rembrandt's great creations.

Strangely enough, it is a face of sorrow. One can easily believe that this man has been in hell, for the traces of suffering have not yet been obliterated by the heavenly life. And yet there is something more in the face than memory of the past. There seems to be a present sorrow. . . . As in a former time he is marveling at their unbelief, for to his own soul the leadings of Providence are so luminously clear. . . .

This is the message of Rembrandt: The death and resurrection of Jesus are not the consummation of his work, but only the commencement. Set free now from the limitations of time and place, he must begin that vaster work which stretches out before his vision till the last syllable of recorded time, the task of bringing a universe to God! The weariness and pain of it are at this moment uppermost; yet even now he fixes his eyes on that far-off divine event toward which he knows the whole creation moves; and breaking the bread of life to these two doubting ones, he vanishes to renew the task with others who need him. And these two will rise at once, return whence they came, and begin their part in the salvation of the world.

— Albert E. Bailey[65]

✳ O God, Whom No One Has Seen

O God, whom no one has seen, we have caught thy reflection in the face of Jesus Christ. We know that thou dost love us, because of the love that he bore to all. Wherever he saw suffering, he had compassion; wherever he saw sinfulness, he brought forgiveness; wherever he saw beauty, he gave thee thanks.

We also would give thee thanks for all that Jesus saw and for the vision he shared with us. Open our eyes that we may never lose sight of thy way for humankind. Awaken us to the sinfulness within our own hearts. Help us to share Jesus' compassion for the unloved and his gratitude for that which is lovely. Show us the vision of thy kingdom, and grant that we may be worthy citizens in it. These things we pray in Jesus' name. Amen.

— **J.M.B.**

✳ Deepen Our Sorrow

Deepen in us now, O God, our sorrow that we have so often followed our Lord but afar off. Open our eyes to see him dying innocent for us who are so full of fault. Grant that by his passion, we may be led to put away those sins which make us unworthy to be numbered among his disciples. By thy redeeming love and saving grace let the shadow of his cross fall upon our lives to make us from this day forward ever mindful of his great and saving love for us. Amen.[66]

✳ Almighty God, Who Hast Shown Us

Almighty God, who hast shown us in the life and teaching of Jesus the true way of blessedness, thou hast also showed us in his suffering and death that the path of love may lead to the cross, and the reward of faithfulness may be a crown of thorns. Give us grace to learn these hard lessons. May we take up our cross and follow Christ, in the strength of patience and the constancy of faith; and may we have such fellowship with him in his sorrow, that we may know the secret of his strength and peace, and see, even in our darkest hour of trial and anguish, the shining of the eternal light. Amen.[67]

✳ Thou, Who Hast Caused the Earth

O thou, who hast caused the earth to bring forth her harvests that bread may be broken for the body, and who renewest the rivers of water that those who are athirst may drink and live; break for our souls' health the bread of life that we may not perish, and pour into us the water of life that we may stoop down and drink unto life eternal. This we ask for his sake whose body was broken and whose life was poured out for us; even Jesus Christ, our Lord. Amen.

— **Boynton Merrill**[68]

✳ The Power for Christian Living

O God, may the power for Christian living, released in the world by the glorious resurrection of our Lord, be felt in the lives of all thy children. Not only at the Easter season, but every day, cause our hearts to be bright with the undimmed light that shines through the centuries from the open tomb, out of which the Master came forth in newness of life. Let no redeemed child of God live in darkness, or gloom, or sin, but may all who are called by thy name keep themselves in the glorious light of thy love; for Jesus' sake. Amen.

— **Stuart G. Oglesby**[69]

Personhood

"Who am I?" This is not the guess-my-name game for dull parties, nor the desperate search for identity of the person afflicted with amnesia, but the quest for self-understanding and for a sense of purpose. "Who am I?" is the common search of nearly every young person.

That question is just beneath the surface in many classroom discussions and in the back of students' minds as homework is done. School is more than pumping facts into a reservoir called a brain. Education helps us discover how to create a happy and constructive life. Similarly, young people are experimenting with answers to that question whenever—and however—they relate to their parents.

Worship is another place in which young people deal with their personhood. "Who am I . . . not only in terms of life goals, but who am I in relation to other people and to the world itself?" It is, in fact, a profoundly theological question. Perhaps worship is the most important place for dealing with it.

✳ Scripture Readings

Am I my brother's (and sister's) keeper — Genesis 4:2b–10
Let no one despise your youth — 1 Timothy 4:11–16
Be strong in the Lord — Ephesians 6:10–18
Avoid conformity — Romans 12
Look not only to your own interests — Philippians 2
You know me, O God — Psalm 139

✳ Hymns

"Lord, I Want to Be a Christian"
"Be Thou My Vision"
"Now in the Days of Youth"
"Make Me a Captive, Lord"
"Awake My Soul, Stretch Every Nerve"
"Lord, Speak to Me"
"Take My Life and Let It Be"

✳ When I'm Feeling Lonely

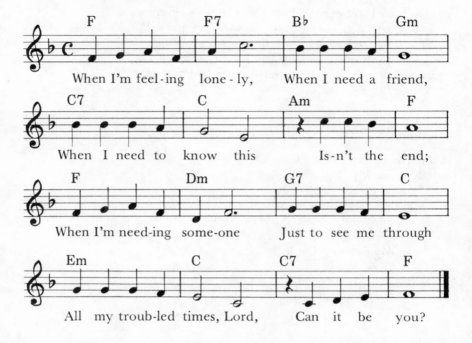

When I'm feel-ing lone-ly, When I need a friend,
When I need to know this Is-n't the end;
When I'm need-ing some-one Just to see me through
All my troub-led times, Lord, Can it be you?

There are lots of times, Lord, When I
  want to pray,
But I don't know how to. What should
  I say?
Do you really listen To each person's
  prayer?
If I find the words, Lord, Will you be
  there?

I've heard people say, Lord, How you
  cared so much
That you sent us Jesus To keep in
  touch.
So we'll follow him, Lord, Hoping that
  it's true;
And thru him we all can Keep close to
  you.

I've got lots of questions I want
  answers for;
Tho I've asked a couple, I've plenty
  more.
If my prayers are answered, If my
  dreams come true,
Lord, are you the reason? Can it be
  you?

I believe you care, Lord, And watch
  over me,
Even tho I wonder Where you can
  be.
I have learned to trust in Everything
  you do.
Since you sent us Jesus, I come to
  you.

This is a personal Hymn . . . best done in a softly rocking style . . . with
guitars and a tender piano descant over gentle, questioning brushes on
a hi-hat or snare drum . . .

— **Richard K. Avery and Donald S. Marsh**[70]

■ 162 ■

✳ A Litany of Faith and Courage

LEADER: O God of Abraham and Sarah, you have led your people in the past; lead us now.

PEOPLE: Grant us the courage of Ruth to leave behind the old and familiar, the courage of Noah to risk laughter and scorn, the hope of Jeremiah to invest in the future, and the unselfishness of Esther to take risks on behalf of others.

LEADER: O God of Moses and Miriam, you delivered your people and led them through the wilderness, giving them food, protection, and guidance.

PEOPLE: In the words of Miriam, we praise you: "I will sing to Yahweh, who has triumphed gloriously!"

LEADER: O God of Deborah and Gideon, you have given us leaders to bring us back when we wander from you, and deliverers to lead us against oppression.

PEOPLE: Give us leaders and deliverers, and grant us the wisdom to follow them.

LEADER: From the words of your prophets we have learned justice and mercy.

PEOPLE: Help us to say, with Isaiah, "Here am I. Send me."

LEADER: O God of James and John and Mary Magdalene, you have called us to follow Jesus.

PEOPLE: Teach us how to work together in mutual responsibility, side-by-side, neither tagging behind nor shoving to the front.

LEADER: O God of Paul and Priscilla and Aquila, who risked their lives for the sake of spreading your church, fill us with enthusiasm for your church.

PEOPLE: Use us in the spreading of the church, in the building up of its parts, in the joining together of its various congregations, and in ministry to the whole world.

LEADER: O God of our Lord Jesus Christ, who gave himself in love for the whole world, teach us so to love.

PEOPLE: Grant us the spirit of Christ, who came not to be served but to serve. Amen.

— **Marilee Scroggs**[71]

✳ Discovering the Real Me
Reading in the form of a prayer

I want to be human, God!
>It's that simple, yet so complex.

I want to be accepted for who I am,
>but something always seems to get in the way—
>my looks, my personality, my view of life,
>my own lack of self-confidence, all aided
>by the bias and indifference of others.

I want to be able to do something no one else can do,
>but the crowd scorns those who differ,
>besides I'm not sure of my abilities—
>what if I fail?

I want to have some say over what's going to happen to me,
>but so often I feel that school and family and
>authority fence me in, and no one seems to care
>what I myself think about my own destiny.

I want to do what's right,
>but how can I know right from wrong
>when even those who should know don't know?
>My parents seem to live in another world,
>the church pussyfoots as society's conscience,
>and leaders make decisions based on popularity, not
>morality.

I want to understand the world around me,
>but things are changing so fast;
>the boom in knowledge numbs my mind,
>fleeting friendships beg for instant intimacy,
>and people mess up nature so that nothing's
>natural anymore.

I want to do something to help others,
>but I don't know how to express my caring without
>making things worse, and when I do see others in need,
>the problem is so big and confusing, I don't know where
>to start. What can I—one human being—do?

O God, I grope for whatever help you can give.

In the reflections of your image, can I find what it is
that makes me human?

In the practice of your love, will my life be fuller, will other
hearts be opened, will broken relationships be healed?

In the variety of your creation, is there truly no one else
quite like me?

Within the order of your universe, is there freedom for me to
be myself if I'm responsible?

In the life of your Son, can I see the way you meant to be right
for me?

In the nature of things around us, is there a balance that is
healthy, a time needed for growing, a sense of justice that
can guide us in knowing what to do to make things better?

In feeling deeply the needs of others, is this the big step in
knowing the humanity in others—and even in
discovering the real me?

— **Herman C. Ahrens, Jr.**[72]

✳ Life
Reading

The temptation is always to reduce it to size. A bowl of cherries. A rat
race. Amino acids. Even to call it a mystery smacks of reductionism. It
is *the* mystery.

As far as anybody seems to know, the vast majority of things in the
universe do not have whatever life is. Sticks, stones, stars, space—they
simply *are*. A few things *are* and are somehow aware of it. They have
broken through into Something, or Something has broken through into
them. Even a jellyfish, a butternut squash. They're in it with us. We're
all in it together, or in us. Life is *it*. Life is *with*.

After lecturing learnedly on miracles, a great theologian was asked
to give a specific example of one. "There is only one miracle," he
answered. "It is life."

Have you wept at anything during the past year?
Has your heart beat faster at the sight of young beauty?
Have you thought seriously about the fact that someday you are going to
die?

More often than not do you really *listen* when people are speaking to you instead of just waiting for your turn to speak?

Is there anybody you know in whose place, if one of you had to suffer great pain, you would volunteer yourself?

If your answer to all or most of these questions is No, the chances are that you're dead.

— Frederick Buechner[73]

✻ Awaken the Life Within Us
Reading in the form of a prayer

O God,
awaken the life within us and around us,
and help us to live life to its fullest.

Life is you and me and everyone else.
Life is always growing, always reaching.
Life is free to be who we are meant to be.
Life is time to do and to become.
Life is pulse and rhythm.
Life is loving and being loved.
Life is knowing and being known.
Life is being heard and hearing others.
Life is healing.
Life is enough food to eat.
Life is work you're proud to do.
Life is making mistakes.
Life is the unknown.
Life is wisdom.
Life is crying.
Life is laughing.
Life is hope.
Life is anger and aggressiveness.
Life is restraint and control.
Life comes in all colors—all beautiful.
Life is no two alike.
Life is a feeling that there is something
bigger than life.

ALL
O God,
help us to know the fullness of life
for ourselves and for others. Amen.

— Herman C. Ahrens, Jr.[74]

✳ It's Almost as If There Were Two Me's
Reading in the form of a prayer

> Something strange happened today, God.
> I was sitting—thinking—being—wrapped around by the
> Music I was listening to when my father walked past and
> rumpled my hair. Rumpled it as if I were a dog or a little kid.
> I almost jerked my head away.
> God, I wanted to hit him. To punch and to smash. Silently
> I screamed, "Leave me alone! I am not your possession,
> not your pet, but ME, an independent person."
> I've never felt so violent before.
> With every nerve tight, I buried myself deeper in the music.
> Eyes closed, ignoring the hand. "Cool it, baby, cool it."
> But inside the churning and shaking wouldn't stop.
> Another thing that bothers me is that for an instant his
> hand felt warm, almost comfortable on my head. I wanted
> to look up and smile, maybe even touch his wrist, but then
> I just wanted to hit, to separate my head from that hand.
> How can I have such opposite feelings at the same time?
> It's almost as if there were two me's.
> I've had another thought that makes things even more
> confusing. What if my father really felt lonely or something
> and was touching me to get some warmth or comfort. I
> can't even sort out my own emotions—how can I cope with
> someone else's needs?
> O God, when will I be able to respond in situations as me—
> one person—not a shell hiding a tangle of conflicting and
> sometimes violent emotions, but me, sure of who I am?
> — **Brenda Reimer**[75]

✳ Help Me Keep My Dreams Alive
Reading in the form of a prayer

In a world of conflict and confusion,
Help me to keep my dreams alive, O God.

I dream of good health.

> Help me to be a worthy steward of the body which you have given
> me. May I never let my health suffer from personal neglect or
> injurious excess.

I dream of always being liked.

> Help me to be a true friend. And no matter how lonely I become
> when I'm away from home, never let me cast aside lifelong
> standards in exchange for shallow acceptance.

I dream of a happy home.

Help me to see what it takes to be a good parent. May I never let silly infatuation, physical appearances, or momentary pleasure blur my understanding of that kind of love for a person that grows and lasts for a lifetime.

I dream of success in a job.

Help me to have confidence in my abilities, but also to know my limitations. May success never be mine if it is achieved by exploiting others.

I dream of right winning over wrong.

In the fight for justice and truth, help me to know what's right. When I am wrong, help me to be big enough to admit my error. When I am right, help me to know how best to change what's wrong.

I dream of a world at peace.

Help me always to be deeply sensitive to the humanness of my neighbor. When I am hungry, rejected, sick, uninformed, poor, or treated as less than human, it is hard for me, too, to live in harmony with others.

O God, help me keep my dreams alive.

— **Herman C. Ahrens, Jr.**[76]

✳ Give Me the Courage
Prayer

On this day, Lord, give me the courage to live one day at a time. I have such high personal ideals; but I sacrifice them just to get by. I think of myself as friendly and outgoing; yet I discover how cross I can be with others close to me. I can define the word "love," but I have so little control over myself in loving others. Lord, one day's faith at a time is enough; not everything about me can be resolved at once. Increase my faith so that I may take new steps of love. Give me strength for today. Amen.

✳ A Place for Me
Prayer

O Lord of earth and heaven, can it be that there is a place for me in your plan for all life? Can it be that there is a work for me to do, and if I fail you will have to wait until someone else can be found? If this is true, guide me until I find my task, and strengthen me to give my life to it. Amen.

Parents, Friends, and School

Emotions strongly felt and expressed are normal for young people. And, because of the importance of parents, friends, and school in their lives, each is likely to prompt deep feelings.

The search for both independence and lasting relationships is the stuff of such expressions. Many young people who are caught up in their encounters with peers and adults want to reflect on the meaning of friendship and seek to put their thoughts into a broader perspective. The resources in this section are designed to help that to happen.

✳ Scripture Readings

Forbearing one another in love — Colossians 3:12–25
What God has joined together — Mark 10:2–9
Be strong in the Lord — Ephesians 6:10–18
A model of friendship — John 15:11–17
The friendship of David and Jonathan — 1 Samuel 13–2 Samuel 1:26

✳ Hymns

"For the Beauty of the Earth"
"Where Cross the Crowded Ways of Life"
"God of Grace and God of Glory"
"What a Friend We Have in Jesus"
"Lord, I Want to Be a Christian"
"Now in the Days of Youth"

✳ A Student's Hymn

For use as a reading or sung to the tune of Materna *("O Beautiful for Spacious Skies")*

Creator of the universe,
We lift our minds to thee;
Enlighten them and lead our thought
In fearless liberty.
Let not our search for truth in things
From thee our souls divide;
Thou art the living Lord of truth;
Thy Spirit be our guide!

When minds are dulled with studying,
When words no life afford,
When fields of knowledge seem too vast,

Sustain us then, O Lord.
Let not the love of easy ways
Leave deeper truth unknown;
Teach us that power to learn and grow
Is found in thee alone.

Make every desk an altar, Lord;
Our studying a prayer;
The classroom doors cathedral gates
To those who enter there.
Let science find in thee its truth;
Technology, its goal;
Philosophy, its noblest thought:
Thy light makes knowledge whole!

— J. Donald Hughes[77]

✳ A Litany for Growth

Because you have planned for us to grow up into the measure of the fullness of the stature of Christ,

Help us to grow today, O God.

In depth of feeling and in self-control,

Help us to grow today, O God.

In our willingness to accept responsibility and to share our time for the good of others,

Help us to grow today, O God.

In concern for the happiness of others, and in ability to see and do things which will contribute to their happiness,

Help us to grow today, O God.

In choosing the best in leisure activities,

Help us to grow today, O God.

In our spiritual understanding and in the closeness of our relationship to you,

Help us to grow today, O God.

In appreciation for those who are different from ourselves, but also in strong loyalty to what we believe to be right,

Help us to grow today, O God.

In the strength and beauty of holiness, and into the likeness of Jesus;

Help us to grow today, O God.

— Lois Horton Young[78]

✳ Jesus at Home
Meditation

When we turn our thoughts to Jesus' childhood and his home life in Nazareth, we are likely to think of him growing up as a solitary child, learning at his mother's knee, helping his father in the carpenter shop, and playing out in the fields with other children from the town. It is hard to imagine him as being exposed to the rough-and-tumble kind of family life that many of us experience in our own homes today. But the Gospels tell us that Jesus was one of many children, and that he learned firsthand about the trials and tribulations of home life.

When we try to picture Jesus as a growing boy, we need to remember that he lived in a house of one, or at most, two rooms, and that there were at least six other children. Very likely the family had only a modest income so that everyone in the family needed to work hard in order to make ends meet. When later in his teaching he used the example of the futility of patching an old garment with new unshrunken cloth, he must have recalled the old days when his own clothing bore many a patch. His story of the woman searching for a lost coin also carried a note of sympathy as coming from one who knew firsthand a household's need for every bit of money.

As the oldest of seven children, Jesus must have had to do his share of baby-sitting at home. Perhaps it was there that his great love of children developed, his gift of making children feel at ease with him.

When from the cross Jesus said to the disciple whom he loved, who was standing near Mary, Jesus' mother, "Behold your mother!" he was giving the last full measure of earthly affection to his mother whom he had loved and reverenced ever since his baby days. In a time when women were usually regarded as being no better than slaves, Jesus' thought for his mother and his gestures of respect toward all women were evidence of a new respect for the position of women that would endure to our own time.

Undoubtedly, too, the joy that Jesus took in weddings and other celebrations, he first learned in his home, where religious festivals and feasts were carefully observed according to devout Jewish custom.

Where but in his home and in his father's carpenter shop could Jesus have come to know the love of a boy for his father, and of a father for a son, so that he could teach us, his followers, to think of God as our loving Father?

Jesus must have valued his home, for he remained there until he was thirty. There he knew, even as young people do today, the worries, the jealousies, which are always a part of home life, however ideal; and the love and reconciliation which can resolve these difficulties for any family member who will try to exercise something of the sympathy and forgiveness that Jesus must have shown in his home as he grew "in wisdom and stature and in favor with God and all people."

— B.J.B. and J.M.B.

✳ I Wonder About My Parents
Poem

> I wonder sometimes when I look at my parents, God,
>   what I'm going to be like when I get married
>   and become a parent myself.
> I may be wrong, but as I watch them,
>   they sometimes seem unsure and overwhelmed by it all.
>
> They're usually polite to each other,
>   but my mom seems to laugh more
>   when she's with other women,
>   my dad seems to light up more
>   when he's "talking business" with other men.
>
> They seem to have made their responsibilities
>   into such heavy weights.
> They both seem to be tired all the time.
> I get the feeling they sometimes
>   avoid each other, avoid me,
>   avoid anything that might make
>   them share from their depths.
>
> Oh, they've given a lot to me as their child,
>   but as I grow older,
>   they seem more uncomfortable
>   and treat me as if I'm still a child,
>   and as I make more of my own decisions,
>   they seem more anxious
>   to give all the right answers.
> They seem caught between holding on to me
>   and letting me grow.
>
> I know they still love me,
>   because when we argue and get angry,
>   they're quick to forgive, and so am I,
>   and when we talk about the future,
>   they say they'll stick by me.
> But love does not always make things easier
>   for them or for me.
> I guess none of us wants to disappoint the other.

They've done a good job of raising me,
    but as I look at them, I wonder
Is what I see now what I have to look forward to?
I wonder,
Do they ever lie in bed and deeply talk
    about intimate things?
Do they ever talk about you, God, and
    share their doubts and uncertainties
    as well as their faith?
Do they ever cry together,
    do they ever spend long times in silence
    where words aren't necessary?
Do they even make love any more
    and if they do
    is that tired and routine like everything else?

They kid each other sometimes,
    about the way my dad falls asleep
    in front of the television,
    about the way my mom talks
    for hours on the phone.
But do they still have loving memories,
    and if they do,
    do they share them with each other
    and would they share some of them with me?

I'd like more often to talk real deeply with them,
    ask them personal questions
    about what happens to love,
    about what scares them,
    about what they think of me.
I'd like to tell them how I see them,
    wonder with them about their lives and mine.

God, help me to help them
    to share more deeply with me and with each other,
    to clear the dust of confusion and
    to ease the weight of responsibility,
    to let them know I care about them,
    to renew the love and joy that once lit our household.
They've given a lot to me,
    maybe I can give something more to them.

Help me, O God, to learn from my parents.
    When I get married,
    don't let walls grow
    between me and my spouse,

between me and my kids,
walls that grow
by the casual piling up of dust
on a once-treasured relationship,
dulling the gift of love that is yours.

I'll bet my parents didn't think it would
happen to them,
just as I don't think it will happen
to me.
But as I look at them,
even with your help,
I wonder.

— **William W. Finlaw**[79]

✳ Triumph Over the Torrent
Reading

The sun beat down on the mountainsides. Among the shaded roots of
the evergreen forest, the winter's snow melted, seeping down through
the soil, becoming trickles and streams.

It was the first hot day of spring. I was working on a forest survey
in the wilderness behind Kitimat in northern British Columbia, tallying
timber for a planned pulp mill.

Gordie Bradshaw and I left camp that morning and waded across
the cold, clear river to the other side. All through the day, as we
worked, the snow peaks above shimmered in the heat; we heard the
run off tinkling musically to join the river below.

When we returned to the river ourselves, at evening, it had
changed. The water that had barely reached our knees in the morning
now raged down, roaring towards the canyon.

"Upstream!" Gordie bellowed in my ear. "The river's wider there. We
might get across!"

Up to our waists in icewater, falling, holding each other up, we
struggled across three channels of rapids. We stumbled onto the last
gravel bar before the far shore. There was only one channel left.

It ran deep and black — too deep to wade, too swift to swim.

Gordie looked at a tree across the channel. "If someone would fell that
tree, we could let the current swing us across on it," he dreamed.

Downstream, a long-dead tree trunk hung out into the current,
which curled past it in an oily boil of angry water. "If we could get hold of
that snag . . ." I suggested.

He looked at me.

I looked at him.

■ 174 ■

We both looked downstream, to where our channel met the crashing chaos at the head of the canyon.

And we looked at our gravel bar, steadily shrinking as the flood kept rising.

I recall mumbling
"One of us has to try it."
Then I stepped in.

The current, stronger than I had expected, whirled me away. The snag came hurtling towards me. For a ghastly second, I thought I would miss it. Then my fingers grabbed it, and I hung on as the water foamed over my head and sluiced through my jacket.

Somehow I wasn't torn loose.

Somehow, I dragged myself onto the log, and to shore.

Gordie hurled our axe across. I began chopping. Minutes later, he waded out the first steps to meet the falling tree, grabbed it, and hauled himself across. As he dripped onto the bank, he hugged me. *"I thought you were a goner,"* he said simply.

Yet if I hadn't tried the torrent, he would have.

There's an old saying: *"Death makes cowards of us all."* We learned that evening that it's not true. Only *useless* death does.

We didn't talk about it, out there on the gravel bar, but Gordie and I both knew the risks. And we knew the effort had to be made. So we did it.

All through history, other people have done as I did. In wars, in disasters, in sudden tragedies, people have discovered unexpected strength, refusing to be scared off their vision, their cause, their commitment, even by the fear of death.

If the prospect of death had made a coward out of Jesus, there would be no Christians today.

— Jim Taylor[80]

✳ When School Is a Bore
Reading

It's the same old thing day after day. Listening to lectures. Memorizing dates and data and formulae. No learning to think things through. Always crummy kids. No talking with teachers as friend to friend. Dissecting "literature" from the long-dead past. Studying science outdated by this morning's headlines. Training for a vocation soon to be doomed by automation. Cramming for exams. Others cheat, while I sweat! And always my parents pushing me when I want to be free, and then not caring when I need them most.

SOMETIMES I GET FED UP WITH SCHOOL!

O God, help me to rise above the temptations of the moment and to see the bigger purpose which the present often hides.

I want to be grown-up, but I'm still growing. I want to do what's right, but I'm not yet sure of right and wrong. I want to be accepted for what I am, but who am I? I need to know so much more before the fullness of life is mine. Is not school my time for getting ready? O God, help me to make the most of it.

From the daily routine at school, help me to find a pattern of life.

From my mixing with all types of people, help me to grow in understanding of myself and human nature.

From hours of study and lecture, help me to learn the disciplines of creative listening and informed thinking in my endless search for truth.

From men and women of ages past and events in the headlines today, help me to grasp a concept of humanity that will shape my perspective for facing the future.

From the maze of activities and assignments, help me to mold a mature sense of responsibility.

From the hypocrisy and confusion of today, help me to sift right from wrong and gain confidence in the right.

From the fast pace of today's living, help me to equip myself to meet the challenge of change, to find security in that which does not change, and to avoid being blindly swept along with the crowd.

From my "teachers" at home, at school, at church, and in the community, help me to firm a foundation for a life fitting to be called Christian.

— **Herman C. Ahrens, Jr.**[81]

✳ Flight 459
Reading

DAUGHTER: Well, here we are. Thanks, Mom.
        (College. Thanks Mom, Good-bye.)

MOTHER: Let's stop in the airport snackbar and grab a bite to eat.
        (I can't wait to get away from here!)

DAUGHTER: (Well I can't wait till you go!)

MOTHER: Can't you finish?

DAUGHTER: I'm not very hungry.

MOTHER: Excited?

DAUGHTER: Yes.
        (No, scared. Mom, I'm gonna miss you. I'm sorry.
        Don't make me go. Mom, I love you.)

MOTHER: Let's go down to the gate.

DAUGHTER: O.K.

MOTHER: You don't want to miss your plane, do you?

DAUGHTER: No. (*Smile. Fake laugh.*)
(When are you leaving?)

MOTHER: (Don't worry, not soon enough!)

DAUGHTER: (You're already too late!)

MOTHER: Seat 24c is in the aisle by the wing. Sir, can't you get her a window seat with a better view?

DAUGHTER: (Mom, my guardian angel. Am I leaving or are you?
Tell me you'll miss me. Take my hand now.)

MOTHER: We have a while to wait till boarding.

DAUGHTER: I don't mind, Mother. I have some reading to do.
(I want to talk to you but what can I say?
Forgive me, I have been ungrateful, impertinent, and selfish. My throat cages the words.)

MOTHER: Flight 459 boarding at Gate 16. Time to go, dear.
(Go. Go where? Away. From what?)

DAUGHTER: Well, good-bye, Mom. (*Quick kiss on the cheek.*)
Thanks for everything.
(Thanks. Eighteen years. Thanks.
The crowd surges forward. I am just one brown bobbing head in a crowd. Alone.
Mom! Wait!
The plane swallows me up.
I sit by the window
watching
a lonely woman crying
watching me.)

— **Leslie Anne Weishaar** [82]

Prayer

There is nothing more personal than prayer. Therefore, many young people find it difficult to talk about prayer.

Ironically, there is also nothing more corporate than prayer. That is, when a group is earnestly caught up in common prayer, the members feel truly one.

Prayer can be very comforting and very comfortable. And it can also be — sometimes at the same time — troubling and strange. It is possible to divide prayers into categories, such as confession and petition and adoration. But prayer is virtually impossible to explain, except in poetry, song, and metaphor. There are several attempts to explain prayer in the readings in this section.

You can learn to pray the way you learn to walk — only by doing it. In the long run, it doesn't help much just to read *about* prayer or to follow someone's how-to-do-it recipe. Therefore, in this section there are just a few suggestions. Beyond these, we invite you to read and listen carefully to the prayers of others. And, above all, to pray and to write your own prayers.

✳ Readings

The Lord's Prayer — Matthew 6:5–15
Jesus in Gethsemane — Luke 22:39–46
Two people at prayer — Luke 18:9–14
Let us worship and bow down — Psalm 95:1–7
Sacrifice acceptable to God — Psalm 51:12, 15–17
Bless the Lord, O my soul — Psalm 103
Create in me a clean heart — Psalm 51

✳ Hymns

"Breathe on Me, Breath of God"
"Have Thine Own Way, Lord"
"Just as I Am, Thine Own to Be"
"Spirit of God, Descend Upon My Heart"
"I Need Thee Every Hour"
"Lord, Speak to Me"
"My Faith Looks up to Thee"

✳ Call to Worship

Dearly beloved, in the holy quiet of this hour, let us draw nigh to the one who heareth prayer; let us remember that God listeneth more to our hearts than to our words.

✳ Offertory Sentence

As we have prayed in our hearts, so now let our prayers be in our deeds.

✴ Benediction

The Lord bless us and keep us:
The Lord make God's face to shine
 upon us, and be gracious to us:
The Lord lift up God's countenance
 upon us, and give us peace (Num. 6:24–26, adapted).

✴ What Prayer Is Not
Meditation

Prayer is not primarily asking God for something. The question so often heard, "Does God answer prayer?" implies that asking is the chief thing about praying. But that is not the case at all. See how much asking is contained in the prayer which Jesus gave his disciples as a model for them to follow. The Lord's Prayer begins by speaking to God, and about God. We say that God's name is to be held in reverence. We express the great hope of the coming of the kingdom, and the doing of God's will on earth as in heaven. Not until we are halfway through do we express any petitions at all, and these are of a most general sort. We ask for our daily bread, which means not merely a loaf of bread but all that we need for our day-to-day existence. We ask that God will forgive us our sins, as we forgive those who sin against us. And we ask that we be not led into any more temptation than we can stand. That is all! Then our thoughts turn back to God once more, and we acknowledge that the kingdom, and the power, and the glory belong to the Almighty forever.

There is nothing here in the way of a request that tomorrow may be a nice day for the Sunday school picnic; or that we may get a job we are hoping for very much; or even that such and such a sick person may be made well. Certain phrases of this sort we would hesitate to insert into the Lord's Prayer. They don't seem to belong to it. The Lord's Prayer is not primarily about us at all; it is chiefly about God.

This is not to say that God is necessarily displeased if we ask for this or that occasionally. God knows that we are just children, and God may be glad to have us make requests, even when we have the wrong things in mind and in our speech. A little fellow may run to his father, asking for the moon which hangs bright in the sky. The father does not argue with his boy or become angry at him, even if the request is out of order. The father smiles at him, pats him on the head, and the two are closer together than they were before. Thus it may be with God and us. But our requests, beseeching God to do something for us or for the world, are scarcely necessary. God already knows about our needs. And God is already doing all that is possible. If God is like a parent, we can scarcely imagine greater efforts based upon our request. The main point of prayer does not lie in asking.

— **Nevin C. Harner**[83]

✳ Prayer for Others
Reading

Many people have less difficulty in believing in prayer for themselves than they do in prayer for others. The possible exception is when that other we pray for is one bound closely to us in family ties or bonds of friendship. When we do hold up before God the life and needs of another, then can come a real sense of what it means to share in God's work and concern.

A famous college dean told how he prayed to God to help students who desperately needed help, and named each student by name before God. Later there came the new insight through the prayer itself and he began to pray: "Lord, help me to know how to help John, and Frank, and Joe." In intercessory prayer one seldom ends where one begins. Have you ever felt and known a difference in your own life because an individual person or a group of persons prayed for you?[84]

✳ The Great Stone Face
Meditation

A good analogy of prayer is Nathaniel Hawthorne's story of the Great Stone Face. You may recall the details of the story. Looking down upon a remote and peaceful valley was the outline of a strong and gentle face, traced out in huge rocks on a mountainside. A legend, which went back to the times of the Indians, promised that a child would be born in this neighborhood who in his manhood would be the precise image of the Great Stone Face. The central character of the story is a boy named Ernest, who grew into manhood within sight of the Great Stone Face. From his mother he heard the famous legend, and many an hour at twilight he would gaze at the rocky countenance on the mountainside, and wonder when the human likeness of the Face would appear. Three times in succession, men who had been born in the valley and gone forth to make a name in the world, returned and were hailed widely as the fulfillment of the legend. The first was Mr. Gathergold, a man of great wealth. The next was Old Blood-and-Thunder, a famous general. And the last was Old Stony Phiz, a successful politician. But each time Ernest looked in vain to find in these men a resemblance to the Face on the mountain. By now Ernest was an old man, widely known for his kindliness and wisdom. He had become unofficial pastor and preacher to the valley, and people came from afar to consult him. It was a poet who had the discernment finally to see that Ernest himself carried the exact resemblance of the Great Stone Face. He had lived in its presence so steadily, that its likeness had been stamped upon him. That is what we mean by prayer.

— **Nevin C. Harner**[85]

■ 180 ■

✳ The Lord's Prayer
Dialogue Meditation

(The leader stands at the front of the room. The Scoffer may speak from anywhere in the audience. The leader actually prays the portion of the prayer in spite of the interruptions from the Scoffer. As the leader begins the prayer, the Scoffer speaks up quickly so as to make the opening question an actual interruption. The speakers are impatient with each other, but they grow in understanding as the leader begins to realize that the Scoffer has a point, until, at the end, each makes a genuine effort to help the other gain new insight.)

LEADER: "Our Father . . ."

SCOFFER: *(belligerently)*: What do you mean, "Our Father"?

LEADER: Why, I mean God. God, the Creator of the universe. God, who made us in God's own image.

SCOFFER: What image? Is God black or white or yellow?

LEADER: The Bible just says that Adam and Eve were created in the image of God. I guess color doesn't matter to God.

SCOFFER: Well, as a South African, it matters to me. I'm speaking for people of color. You are hypocritical when you say *"Our* Father." If God created all of us, that makes us brothers and sisters, doesn't it? Would you say your sister can't eat in the same restaurant because her skin is dark?

LEADER: I don't care where you eat!

SCOFFER: Sure you don't care. You don't care where I can't eat. You don't care that there's not enough food to go around, either. You won't *let* me eat—because you don't care enough to do something about it.

LEADER: *(impatiently)*: "Our Father . . ." O.K., now I want to pray.

SCOFFER: There you go again. How can you pray to your God as Father? My father loves me. He provides what I need.

LEADER: So does God. Jesus said, "God is love." God does take care of us. God tries to counsel and guide us. But because we are human beings, created in God's image, we don't have to respond or obey. God helps us—but we often ignore that assistance. God *does* give us what we need. Scientists say that we know how to produce enough of everything the world needs. God gives us that ability. And God gives the sun and rain, the soil and the seed, the strength and the knowledge.

SCOFFER: So why are a third of the people in the world hungry?

LEADER: That's not God's fault. The Bible teaches us to help each other. Jesus taught us to share. God gives, but we don't distribute those gifts very well. We all seem to want to keep what we have. Now let us pray: "Our Father in heaven, hallowed be thy name."

SCOFFER: Wanta know what I think about that? It's crazy to pray to someone millions of miles away. And if you think anyone is going to think your God's name is holy when they are hungry and cold, or despised or lonely, or sick or homeless—well, "holy" isn't what they call God.

LEADER: You don't understand very well. Heaven isn't a place in the sky. Heaven is wherever God is. Heaven is where there's happiness and love.

And God does do something about people's misery. That's why we pray, "Thy kingdom come, thy will be done, on earth as it is in heaven." We know that God wants everyone to be happy and have enough of everything. But God can't *make* us do what is right. God tells us and helps us and nudges us, but God doesn't *make* us do what's right.

SCOFFER: So, why do you ask God to?

LEADER: It isn't just asking. When we pray, we are telling God that we want help and will try to do these things. We don't mean it if we're not willing to help.

SCOFFER: Yeah! What if the kingdom did come—tomorrow! Where would you be? Mighty uncomfortable, I'll bet. Where would you hide your affluence? What would you do with your prejudice? What about the way you buy milk shakes when in Ethiopia and around the world there are babies who don't have milk? Your churches are exclusive little clubs.

LEADER: Maybe we don't act like good citizens of God's kingdom. But we want to be. That's why we are here now. We're trying to become good citizens in God's kingdom. You have some good ideas, though. Like about the hungry people in the world. Why don't you pray with me, "Give us this day our daily bread"?

SCOFFER: *(beginning to be conciliatory):*   That's all right, but you say God has already given it to you. We need to get people to start sharing. The greatest prosperity the country has ever seen—but I guess you are right. That's not God's fault. It's ours.

LEADER: The trouble with us is that we want to save bread for tomorrow and the next day when many people didn't have any at all today. That's why we must pray, "Forgive us our debts, as we forgive our debtors."

SCOFFER: I'd be afraid to pray that. It's hard to forgive. Look at what happens after a terrorist attack. Forgiveness means no grudges, no resentments, no revenge. You really have to love people to pray like that.

LEADER: We don't think about that when we pray, but that's just what Jesus meant. He forgave everyone. Even when they crucified him, he asked God to forgive them. I guess Jesus thought his followers would forgive. If we fail in this, we aren't his followers. But if we do forgive, we don't need to be afraid.

You can be a follower if you pray as he did, "Lead us not into temptation, but deliver us from evil."

SCOFFER: Do you mean that God deliberately tempts you? I have enough trouble with my friends without anything like that.

LEADER: I guess we don't think too much about that, either. God doesn't really tempt us, except that we are always being challenged. I think it's always a temptation not to respond to a challenge—not to live courageously.

Anyway, St. Paul says that no one has a temptation too big to resist. If we are to help God answer this part of our prayer, we need to associate with people who will encourage us to do God's will. We aren't strong enough by ourselves. That's why we say: "For thine is the kingdom, the power and the glory for ever."

SCOFFER: That's strange too. What does it mean?

LEADER: It means that God's kingdom is right here. That God's laws are the laws of life. That the power for good is from God and is available to us. That we should give God the credit—the glory—for whatever we achieve because God made it possible.

SCOFFER: Maybe you're not so hypocritical if you pray that prayer sincerely. Let me pray it with you. And I'll try to help you and God answer it, too.
(Both pray the Lord's Prayer and the group joins in.)

— Adapted from **John H. Huston**[86]

✳ Prayer Is the Soul's Sincere Desire
Prayer

> Prayer is the soul's sincere desire,
> Uttered or unexpressed,
> The motion of a hidden fire
> That trembles in the breast.
>
> Prayer is the burden of a sigh,
> The falling of a tear,

The upward glancing of an eye,
When none but God is near.

Prayer is the simplest form of speech
That infant lips can try,
Prayer, the sublimest strains that reach
The Majesty on high.

O thou by whom we come to God —
The life, the truth, the way —
The path of prayer thyself hast trod,
Lord, teach us how to pray!

— **James Montgomery**[87]

✴ A Litany of Confession

LEADER: Too long, O Lord, have we tried thy patience! Too often have we betrayed the sacred trust thou hast given us to keep; yet still thou art willing that we may come to thee, as we now do, beseeching thee to drown our transgressions in the sea of thine infinite love:
Our failure to be true even to our own accepted standards;
Our self-deception in the face of temptation;
Our choosing of the worse when we know the better;

GROUP: O Lord, forgive.

LEADER: Our failure to apply to ourselves the standards of conduct we demand of others;
Our blindness to the suffering of others, and our slowness to learn from our own suffering;
Our complacency toward wrongs that do not touch our own case, and our oversensitivity to those that do;

GROUP: O Lord, forgive.

LEADER: Our slowness to see the good in others and the evil in ourselves;
Our hardness of heart toward our neighbors' faults, and our readiness to make allowance for our own;
Our unwillingness to believe that thou hast called us to a small work and our brother to a great one.

GROUP: O Lord, forgive. Amen.

✳ A Season of Directed Prayer

(Here the leader suggests a brief prayer thought, and the group prays silently. The leader allows at least fifteen seconds for each period of silent prayer. When the group becomes accustomed to such prayer periods, this interval may be lengthened to thirty seconds, then forty-five seconds, and finally a full minute. Silence is important in worship, but is difficult for an inexperienced leader to handle skillfully.)

LEADER: Let us bow in silent prayer. *(Pause)* Let us give thanks for the world God has created. *(Pause)* Let us give thanks for Jesus Christ, the Son of God, who came that we might know God as our Parent. *(Pause)* Let us give thanks that we are privileged to draw near to God in prayer. *(Pause)*

We give thee thanks, Lord God of our salvation, because thou doest all things for the good of our life, that we may always look steadfastly unto thee, the Savior and Benefactor of our souls, for thou hast refreshed us in the night passed and raised us up, and brought us to worship thy glorious name. We beseech thee to give us grace and power that we may be accounted worthy to sing praise to thee with understanding, and to pray to thee without ceasing. Amen.[88]

The Lord's Supper

Most churches follow their own order of service for Holy Communion. Although they encourage youth and lay people to plan and lead other services of worship, it is almost universally understood that ministers preside at the Lord's Table. Often, however, the liturgy that precedes the consecration and distribution of the bread and wine is creatively developed, and frequently youth or other lay persons lead those parts of the worship.

The materials that follow include segments that could be used in a service that includes the Lord's Supper.

✳ Procession

The eucharistic procession may take place at the beginning of the service or when the offering is presented. If it is at the beginning, an even number of persons carry bread, wine, candles, flowers, and perhaps a Bible to the table. If the communion elements (the bread and wine—sometimes an unbroken loaf of bread and a pitcher of wine) are brought forward as part of the offering, they are presented with the offering plates. When the size of the worshiping congregation permits, the procession may consist of twelve persons, including young women and young men.

✳ Call to Worship

LEADER: Come, believers, and sing your alleluias to God!

ALL: Praise God, who invades our every day with Light
and who ignites each star in our darkness.

LEADER: Praise God, who out of love for us
sent Jesus Christ to live among us.

ALL: So that in our hunger and thirst
we might have Bread and Wine.

LEADER: Come, let us celebrate that God reaches
into the niches of our living and claims us.

ALL: We are God's people;
God is our Lord!

LEADER: We pray that we might be faithful to our covenant,
for in God is life created anew.

ALL: In God is our Sabbath.

LEADER: Come, Holy Spirit, come and find us now
in the wilderness of our beings and lead us forth
out of chaos to God's festival of rainbows.

ALL: Praise God who promises us Shalom!

✳ Preparation

LEADER: Blessed are you, Lord God of the universe,
you are the giver of this bread,
fruit of the earth and of human labor:
let it become the bread of life.

CHOIR (OR CONGREGATION): Blessed be God, now and forever!

LEADER: Blessed are you, Lord God of the universe,
you are the giver of this wine,
fruit of the vine and of human labor:
let it become the wine of the eternal kingdom.

CHOIR: Blessed be God, now and forever!

LEADER: As the grain once scattered in the fields
and the grapes once dispersed on the hillside
are now reunited on this table

in bread and wine,
so, Lord, may your whole church
soon be gathered together
from the corners of the earth into your kingdom.

Various choral responses would be appropriate for use by the choir or congregation. Consider, for example, using the concluding Alleluia from the hymn "From All That Dwell Below the Skies" or the final "Praise God! Praise God, Praise with us the God of grace!" from "Praise, My Soul, the King of Heaven."

✴ Confession of Sin

LEADER: Sisters and brothers, let us confess our sins and ask God for the forgiveness we need.

ALL: We confess that often we have failed to be obedient disciples.
We have not done your will,
We have broken your law,
We have rebelled against your love,
We have not loved our neighbors,
    and we have not heard the cry of the needy.
Forgive us, we pray.
Free us for joyful obedience, through Jesus Christ our Lord.
Amen.

LEADER: Anyone in Christ becomes a new person altogether;
the past is finished and gone.
Everything has become fresh and new.
Friends, believe the good news of the gospel:
    In Jesus Christ, we are forgiven!

✴ A Sign of Peace

LEADER: Dear friends, Jesus taught us, "If you are about to offer your gift to God at the altar, and there remember that your neighbor has something against you, leave your gift in front of the altar, go at once and make peace with your neighbor, and then come back and offer your gift."

ALL: In response to Christ's command, we reach out to one another in love.

✳ **Word of Mission**   *(to be used at the end of the service with the Blessing)*

LEADER: Jesus says, "I am the living bread which has come down from
heaven;
Anyone who eats this bread will live forever:"
Go in peace and serve the Lord.

ALL: Thanks be to God.

✳ **Blessing**

LEADER: The Lord bless you and keep you.
The Lord make God's face shine on you
and be gracious to you.
The Lord look upon you with favor and give you peace.

ALL: Amen.[89]

General Resources

Calls to Worship

✳ The Lord's Day

This is the day which the Lord has made. Let us rejoice and be glad in it. This is a new day, not just another day. The day is rich with the potential and the opportunity for freeing our lives from fear and despair. So, let us come together in that spirit, determined to open our hearts to God's deliverance, in the name of the God who creates us, Jesus who liberates us, and the Spirit who gives us the strength to persevere. Amen.

— **Jerry Paul**[90]

✳ Enter With Thanksgiving

Enter into God's gates with thanksgiving —
    Thanksgiving for life, for health,
    For eyes to see, and ears to hear,
    For folk to love and friends to know,
    For thoughts to think,
    For God to worship.
Enter into God's courts with praise.
For God is good. God's truth endures to
    to all generations.

— Adapted from **Clarice M. Bowman**[91]

✳ Calls to Worship From the Bible

Psalm 37:7, 4	Psalm 95:6–7	Isaiah 52:7a
Psalm 46:1–2a	Psalm 100:2, 4–5	Habakkuk 2:20
Psalm 84:1–2, 4	Isaiah 40:31	John 4:23–24
Psalm 92:1–2		

Prayers of Confession and Assurances of Pardon

✳ An Instrument of Peace

> God, I so want to be an instrument of your peace
>> But instead I am a weapon for war.
>
> Forgive me.
>> My hatred, jealousy, anger, and resentment fester
>> And the powers that lead to war are increased.
>
> God, I so want to be a beacon of your hope
>> But instead I am a fog of despair.
>
> Forgive me.
>> My insecurity, fear, and depression erupt
>> And my hope is quenched in sadness.
>
> God, I so want to be your person
>> But instead I let other forces control me.
>
> Help me I pray. Amen.[92]

✳ Thou, O Lord, Hast Promised

> Thou, O Lord, hast promised:
> That if we will confess our sins
> Thou art faithful and just to forgive us our sins.
> We come in penitence seeking thy forgiveness;
> That we may know the joy of thy presence;
> And the light of thy face.
>
> Thou alone knowest how often we have offended thee;
> And hurt the lives of others.
> Forgive us, O Lord, for every unkind thought;
> Every untrue word;
> Every wrong act.
> Forgive us:
> For we have been selfish;
> And have not thought of the needs of others.
> Forgive us:
> For our ingratitude;
> Our neglect of prayer;
> Our carelessness in the use of money;
> Our forgetfulness of our sacred vows.
> O God, have mercy upon us.
> Create in us clean hearts and renew a right spirit within us.
> For the sake of Jesus Christ our Lord. Amen.[93]

✳ Kyrie

Ky - ri - e e - lei - son, Ky - ri - e e - lei - son,

Ky - ri - e e - le - i - son.

— **Liturgy of the Russian Orthodox Church**[94]

✳ Litany of Confession

LEADER: God, you gave me eyes that I might see.
You sent Christ that my eyes might be opened.
I confess that I have not always used them as they might best
be used.
I looked around me and saw flowers in the field.

PEOPLE: I did not see the weeds and not seeing could not pull them
out.

LEADER: I looked around me and saw health.

PEOPLE: I did not see illness and not seeing could not care or even ease
it.

LEADER: I looked around me and saw joy.

PEOPLE: I did not see unhappiness and not seeing could not
share my friends' unhappiness
or make their burden lighter.

LEADER: I looked around me and saw peace.

PEOPLE: I did not see discontent and not seeing could not find its roots
and remove them from our lives.

LEADER: I looked around me and saw satisfaction.

PEOPLE: I did not see hunger and not seeing could not feed those who
starve.

LEADER: I looked around me and saw friendship.

PEOPLE: I did not see loneliness and not seeing could not extend a
hand.

LEADER: God, make my eyes sighted once more.
Take from me the burden of my failures.
and give me clearer sight that I may truly see need
where it exists and open my eyes to all your people.
Amen.

— Linda Warwick[95]

✳ A Confession

Almighty and most merciful God, we acknowledge and confess that we have sinned against thee in thought, word, and deed; that we have not loved thee with all our heart and soul, with all our mind and strength; and that we have not loved our neighbor as ourselves. We beseech thee, O God, to be forgiving to what we have been, to help us to amend what we are, and of thy mercy to direct what we shall be, so that the love of goodness may ever be first in our hearts and we may follow unto our life's end in the steps of Jesus Christ our Lord. Amen.

— Traditional prayer

✳ Heal Us

Grandfather,
Look at our brokenness.

We know that in all creation
Only the human family
Has strayed from the Sacred Way.

We know that we are the ones
Who are divided
And we are the ones
Who must come back together
To walk in the Sacred Way.

Grandfather,
Sacred One,
Teach us love, compassion, and honor
That we may heal the earth
And heal each other.

— Art Solomon, Ojibway Nation[96]

✳ God Is Our Father

God is our father, who will always welcome us home after we have
 been lost.
God is our mother, whose love will search for us until she finds us.
In Jesus of Nazareth, God is our brother, who gave his life to show us
 love.
God is justice and God is love. This is our assurance of forgiveness
 when we confess our sins.

— **Carol Bernard**[97]

✳ The Good News

The good news in Christ is that when we face ourselves and God with
the awareness of our need, we are given grace to grow, and courage to
continue the journey. Amen.

— **Ruth C. Duck**[98]

The good news is that Christ calls us to new life and enables us to
begin again and again and again. Let us praise God with songs of joy!

— **Ruth C. Duck**[99]

✳ Assurances of Pardon From the Bible

Psalm 34:17–18
Psalm 86:15
Lamentations 3:22–23a
Matthew 11:28–30

Offering Sentences and Prayers

✳ God, We Know

God, we know that
Bread for ourselves is a material question.
Bread for our sisters and brothers is a spiritual question.
May these gifts reflect the spiritual dimensions of our lives.
May they be used to renew the spirits of our brothers and sisters
 throughout your world.
Amen.

— **Jerry Paul**[100]

✻ Three Prayers on Giving

A part of ourselves, we give, O God;
    A part of ourselves we consecrate here,
Claim our whole selves, O God,
    Time, talents, all,
Till our surrendered lives,
    Thy plans fulfill. Amen.

We may give without loving but we cannot love without giving.

We could give thee nothing, O thou great Giver of every good and perfect gift, if thou hadst not first given it to us. Grant us grace so to do with what for the moment is ours, that we may please thee with what is eternally thine. Amen.

— **Traditional prayer**[101]

✻ Offering Sentences From the Bible

Deuteronomy 15:11b	Luke 6:38
Deuteronomy 16:17	2 Corinthians 9:6b–7
Psalm 24:1	Colossians 3:23
Matthew 5:16	

Calls to Prayer and General Prayers

✻ Calls to Prayer From the Bible

Psalm 19:14
Psalm 51:15
Hebrews 4:16
James 4:8a, 10

✻ Give Us Wisdom

Gracious and Holy God,
Give us wisdom to perceive thee,
Diligence to seek thee,
Eyes to behold thee,
A heart to meditate upon thee
    through Jesus Christ our Lord. Amen.[102]

✴ Great Art Thou

Great art thou, O Lord, and greatly to be praised; great is thy power, and thy wisdom is infinite. Thee would we praise without ceasing. Thou callest us to delight in thy praise, for thou hast made us for thyself, and our hearts find no rest until we rest in thee; to whom with the Father and the Holy Spirit, all glory, praise, and honor be ascribed, both now and forevermore. Amen.

— **Augustine**[103]

✴ Defend Us

O Lord, our heavenly Father, almighty and everlasting God, who hast safely brought us to the beginning of this day: defend us in the same with thy mighty power; and grant that this day we fall into no sin; neither run into any kind of danger; but that all our doings may be ordered by thy governance, to do always that which is righteous in thy sight, through Jesus Christ our Lord. Amen.

— **Book of Common Prayer**[104]

Benedictions and Closing Sentences

✴ God Be in My Head

God be in my head, and in my understanding;
God be in my eyes, and in my looking;
God be in my mouth, and in my speaking;
God be in my heart, and in my thinking:
God be at my end, and my departing.

— **Sarum Primer, 1558**[105]

✴ The Spirit of the Living God.

May the Spirit of the Living God . . .
    Be above you to bless you,
    Before you to guide you,
    Behind you to forgive you,
    Beside you to comfort you,
    Beneath you to sustain you,
and continually surprise you with
great love for you each moment
along life's way.

— **Robert G. Kemper**[106]

✳ Go Forth in Peace

Go forth in peace, be led out in joy. Let the mountains and the hills before you break forth into singing. Let the trees and fields clap their hands. Join the celebration of life in the whole creation.

— **Michael Bausch**[107]

✳ God Sends Us

God sends us into the world, to accept the cost and to discover the joy of discipleship. Therefore go — carrying with you the peace of Christ, the love of God, and the encouragement of the Holy Spirit, in trial and rejoicing. Amen.

— **Ruth C. Duck** [108]

✳ God Go With You

> God go with you.
> May God walk where you walk;
> Guide where you must make choices;
> Comfort where you hurt;
> And surprise you by continued love for you
> and what you are
> and what you do. Amen.

— Adapted from **Robert G. Kemper**[109]

✳ You Have Let Me Pass the Day

> O God, you have let me pass the day in peace,
> Let me pass the night in peace.
> O Lord, you have no Lord.
> There is no strength but in you.
> There is no unity but in your house.
> Under your hand I pass the night.
> You are my mother and my father.
> You are my home. Amen.

— **The Boran of Kenya**[110]

✳ Litany of Benediction

LEADER: Go into the world in faith!

PEOPLE: Trusting God to lead you, trusting people to receive you.

LEADER: Go into the world with hope!

PEOPLE: With God's presence before you and human dreams to carry you.

LEADER: Go into the world with love!

PEOPLE: Serving with those in whom Christ lives, and laboring for those for whom Christ died.

LEADER: Go in faith, hope, and love!

— Wheadon United Methodist Church Worship Commission,
Evanston, Ill.[111]

Bibliography

Books About Worship and Approaches to Worship

DeSola, Carla. *Learning Through Dance*. Paramus, N.J.: Paulist/Newman Press, 1974. ■ Solid interpretation of relationship between dance movements and religious ideas.

DeSola, Carla. *The Spirit Moves: A Handbook of Dance and Prayer*. Washington, D.C.: Liturgical Conferences, 1977. ■ Relates dance to the eucharist, Christian seasons, special occasions, and scripture.

Emswiler, Thomas Neufer, and Sharon Emswiler. *Wholeness in Worship: Creative Models for Sunday, Family, and Special Services*. San Francisco: Harper & Row, 1980. ■ A holistic approach to worship with an emphasis on making worship more lively and inclusive.

Harrell, John, and Mary Harrell. *To Tell of Gideon: The Art of Storytelling in the Church*. Berkeley, Calif.: copyright by John and Mary Harrell, 1975. ■ Just what the title says it is.

Harrell, John, and Mary Harrell. *A Storyteller's Treasury*. Berkeley, Calif.: copyright by John and Mary Harrell, 1977. ■ A collection of biblical, folk, and other stories suitable for worship.

Hauck, Allan. *Calendar of Christianity*. Lima, Ohio: C.S.S. Publishing Co., 1975. ■ Background on holidays and holy days.

Litherland, Janet. *The Clown Ministry Handbook*. Colorado Springs, Colo.: Contemporary Drama Service, 1982. ■ A comprehensive book on the subject including techniques, history, biblical background, and how to organize a clown group.

Mossi, John P., ed. *A Study and Planning Guide for Worship*. Paramus, N.J.: Paulist/Newman Press, 1976. ■ A collection of articles from *Modern Liturgy* magazine with a Roman Catholic slant to worship.

O'Day, Rey, and Edward A. Powers. *Theater of the Spirit: A Worship Handbook*. New York: Pilgrim Press, 1980. ■ A practical guide to understanding the meaning of worship.

Sparkman, G. Temp. *Writing Your Own Worship Materials*. Valley Forge, Pa.: Judson Press, 1980. ■ Easy-to-follow suggestions for writing prayers, calls to worship, litanies, etc.

Vienna. *Banners & Mobiles & Odds & Ends; A Book of Simple Decorations.* New York: Morehouse-Barlow Co., 1973. ▪ A creative approach to setting up worship environments. If you want only one book on environment, this is it.

White, James F. *Introduction to Christian Worship.* Nashville: Abingdon Press, 1980. ▪ A thorough but readable textbook on Christian worship for those who want to delve into its history and current developments.

White, Williams R. *Speaking in Stories: Resources for Christian Storytellers.* Minneapolis: Augsburg Publishing House, 1982. ▪ How to use stories in worship and a good collection of stories.

"Toward More Inclusive Language in the Worship of the Church," Community Council of Wesley Theological Seminary, Washington, D.C. 1980. ▪ "Creating a Vision of Life Abundant and Whole Through More Inclusive Language," Lancaster Theological Seminary, Lancaster, Pa., 1982. ▪ These two pamphlets represent some of the best thinking about why to use inclusive language and how to use it.

Books of Prayers, Poetry, and Other Service Materials

Ahrens, Hermans C., Jr., ed. *Keep in Touch: Prayers, Poems, Images and Celebrations by and for the Young.* New York: Pilgrim Press, 1978. ▪ The title says it all.

Ahrens, Herman C., Jr., ed. *Tune In.* New York: Pilgrim Press, 1968. ▪ Prayers for and by youth.

Bell, Martin. *The Way of the Wolf: The Gospel in New Images.* New York: Seabury Press, 1969. ▪ Stories, songs, and poems to bring the gospel story into new and often magical images.

Brandt, Leslie F. *Epistles/Now.* St. Louis: Concordia Publishing House, 1976. ▪ A rewriting of part of the New Testament letters in modern language.

Brandt, Leslie F. *Psalms/Now.* St Louis: Concordia Publishing House, 1973. ▪ A rewriting of the Psalms that captures the essence instead of simply translating the words.

Burgess, Stephen W., and Janes D. Righter. *Celebrations for Today: Acts of Worship in the Modern English Language.* Nashville: Abingdon Press, 1977. ▪ Contemporary worship services.

Duck, Ruth C., ed. *Bread for the Journey.* New York: Pilgrim Press, 1981.

Duck, Ruth C., ed. *Flames of the Spirit.* New York: Pilgrim Press, 1985. ▪ Resources for worship, most of them prepared by contemporary Christians, some adapted from the Bible and traditional sources. In inclusive language.

Gonzalez, Justoc, and Catherine Gonzalez. *In Accord: Let us Worship.* New York: Friendship Press, 1981. ▪ A worship book for those who wish to explore pluralism and multiracial and multicultural resources.

Habel, Norman C. *Hi! Have a Nice Day.* Philadelphia: Fortress Press, 1972. ▪ Free verse for young people along with litanies and readings on the world around us.

Haas, James E. *Praise the Lord!* New York: Morehouse-Barlow Co., 1974. ▪ Eleven services on subjects of interest to youth and built around the Episcopal eucharist. Ideas are adaptable to other worship forms.

Quoist, Michel. *Prayers.* New York: Sheed & Ward, 1963. ▪ Prayers in free verse on everyday subjects.

Richards, Blair, and Janice Sigmund. *Come, Let us Celebrate! A Resource book of Contemporary Worship Services.* New York: Hawthorne Books, W. Clement Stone, Publisher, 1976. ▪ Full text for twenty-six original services in what the authors call new-form worship.

Savary, Louis M., S.J., and Thomas J. O'Connor, eds. *The Heart Has Its Seasons: Reflections on the Human Condition.* New York: Regina Press, 1970. ▪ Photographs, poems, and readings about the varied nature of the human condition.

Simon, Ann, comp. *Heads Bowed Together: Worship Resources on Reconciliation.* New York: Friendship Press, 1966. ▪ Readings, poems, and prayers on reconciliation.

Weems, Ann. *Reaching for Rainbows.* Philadelphia: Westminster Press, 1980. ▪ Poetry, dialogues, choric speech, and full services in an upbeat manner.

Winter, Miriam Therese, *God-With-Us: Resources for Prayer and Praise,* Nashville: Abingdon Press, 1979. ▪ Creative poetry, prose, prayer, and song for praising God. Beginnings, turning points, and returning form the basic structure of this book.

Plays and Musicals

Plays

Baker, Kenneth S. *Dramatic Moments in the Life of Christ,* Atlanta: John Knox Press, 1978. ▪ Multiple copies of seven chancel dramas for three to eight actors.

Habel, Norman, ed. *What Are We Going to Do With All These Rotting Fish? (And Seven Other Short Plays for Church and Community).* Philadelphia: Fortress Press, 1970. ▪ As much for discussion as for worship. Plays in this book have a tendency to be funny rather than serious.

Poovey, W.A. *Mustard Seeds and Wine Skins: Dramas and Meditations on Seven Parables.* Minneapolis: Augsburg Publishing House, 1972. ▪ Parables brought to life with minimum staging and costuming.

Poovey, W.A., *Six Prophets for Today.* Minneapolis: Augsburg Publishing House, 1977. ▪ Simple dramas of the prophets.

Musicals

Godspell. Conceived and originally directed by John-Michael Tebelak, music and new lyrics by Stephen Schwartz. Theatre Maximus, 1650 Broadway, Suite 6091, New York, NY 10019.

Love, You Spoke a Word. Words and music by Ken Medema with dramatic materials by Craig McNair Wilson. GlorySound, Shawnee Press, Delaware Water Gap, PA 18327.

It's Cool in the Furnace. Music by Buryl Red, book and lyrics by Grace Hawthorne. Word Music, 4800 W. Waco Drive, Waco, TX 76710.

Moses and the Freedom Fanatics. By Hal H. Hopson. Choristers Guild, P.O. Box 38188, Dallas, TX 75238.

Songs of Pilgrimage. By Ken Medema. GlorySound, Shawnee Press, Delaware Water Gap, PA, 18327.

The Story-Tellin' Man. By Ken Medema. Word Music, 4800 W. Waco Drive, Waco, TX 76710.

Addresses

Catalogs may be obtained from companies mentioned in the preceding list. In addition the following groups offer plays:

Baker's Plays, 100 Summer Street, Boston, MA 02110.
C.S.S. Publishing Co., 628 South Main, Lima, OH 45804.
Contemporary Drama Service, Box 7710-S4, Colorado Springs, CO 80933.
Samuel French Plays, 45 West 25th Street, New York, NY 10010.

Song Books

Avery and Marsh Songbook. Richard K. Avery and Donald S. Marsh. Port Jervis, N.Y.: Proclamation Productions, 1973. ▪ All new music in a popular vein.

Everflowing Streams. Ed. Ruth C. Duck and Michael G. Bausch. New York: Pilgrim Press, 1981. ▪ Hymns both rewritten and newly written in inclusive language.

Exodus Songbook. Ed. Carlton R. Young. Carol Stream, Ill.: Agape, 1976. ▪ A variety of recent, popular "religious" songs.

Inclusive Language Hymns (Based on The Pilgrim Hymnal, 1958). Amherst Mass.: First Congregational Church, 1984. ▪ Common and traditional hymns rewritten in inclusive language. Well done and poetic.

Joy in Singing. Jane Parker Huber. Louisville, Ky.: Joint Office of Worship, 1044 Alta Vista Road, 1983. ▪ Forty-one totally new hymns set to familiar and traditional tunes.

Lift Every Voice and Sing: A Collection of Afro-American Spirituals and Other Songs. New York: Church Hymnal Corporation, 1981.

Sing to God: Songs and Hymns for Christian Education. Ed. Mary Hawkes and Paul Hamill: New York: United Church Press, 1984. ▪ Hymns for children and youth, both traditional and modern but all in inclusive language.

Sisters and Brothers Sing! Ed. Sharon Emswiler and Tom Neufer Emswiler. Normal, Ill.: Wesley Foundation Campus Ministry, 1977. ▪ Inclusive-language songs but with an additional section of fresh, new worship resources.

Songbook for Saints and Sinners. Ed. Carlton R. Young. Carol Stream, Ill.: Agape, 1971. ▪ New and old songs of a broadly religious nature.

Songs. Comp. Yohann Anderson. San Anselmo, Calif.: Songs & Creations, 1972. ▪ A collection of 580 songs including popular, camp, and religious songs. Available as *The Tune Book* with melody line and guitar chord.

Songs for a New Creation. Minneapolis: Augsburg Publishing House, 1982. ▪ Largely original hymns and service music especially designed for Lutheran young people but usable by all denominations.

Songs of Zion. Nashville: Abingdon Press, 1981. ▪ Black songs and hymns.

The Genesis Songbook. Comp. Carlton R. Young. Carol Stream, Ill.: Agape, 1973. ▪ Mostly modern songs with a few spirituals thrown in.

Calendar of Resources and Index

This calendar is based on a combination of the church's liturgical and program year with regular events. It has cross references to materials in Chapter 14, "Resources for Special Days and Seasons," and Chapter 15, "Topical Resources."

Advent

See Advent resources in Chapter 14.
See resources about Jesus in Chapter 15.

APPROPRIATE SCRIPTURE

The prophecy—Isaiah 40:1–11; 60: 1, 3; 61:1–3; 11:1–4; 9:2–7

Christmas Eve / Christmas Day

See Christmas resources in Chapter 14, page 76 et seq.
See resources about Jesus in Chapter 15, pages 148–160.

APPROPRIATE SCRIPTURE

The birth—Matthew 1:18–2:23; Luke 2:1–38

Watch Night / New Year's Day

See New Year's Eve and New Year's Day resources in Chapter 14, pages 80–83.
If your theme for the New Year is peace, see resources on peace and justice in Chapter 15, pages 99–112.

APPROPRIATE SCRIPTURE

The guardian of Israel never sleeps—Psalm 121
A time to be born, a time to die—Ecclesiastes 3:1–8
Behold, I make all things new—Revelation 21:1–6

Epiphany

See resources on the church's unity and mission in Chapter 15, especially "The Meaning of Mission," page 123.
See resources about Jesus in Chapter 15, pages 148–160.

APPROPRIATE SCRIPTURE

The visit of the Magi and the Great Commission—Matthew 2:1–12; 28:16–20

Martin Luther King, Jr.'s, Birthday

(Resources also appropriate for Lincoln's Birthday.)
See resources on peace and justice in Chapter 15, pages 99–112, especially page 103.
"Confession of sin," page 114
"A Litany for Unity," page 115

APPROPRIATE SCRIPTURE

Let justice roll like waters—Amos 5:21–34
What does the Lord require?—Micah 6:8
What God's servants will do—Isaiah 42:1–6

Boy Scout Sunday / Girl Scout Sunday

See resources on personhood in Chapter 15, pages 160–168.
See resources on parents, friends, and school in Chapter 15, pages 169–177.

APPROPRIATE SCRIPTURE

You know me O God—Psalm 139
Let no one despise your youth—1 Timothy 4:11–16
Be strong in the Lord—Ephesians 6:10–18

Ash Wednesday / Lent

See resources for Lent, Holy Week, and Easter in Chapter 14, pages 83–90.
See resources about Jesus in Chapter 15, pages 148–160.
See resources on prayer in Chapter 15, pages 177–185.

APPROPRIATE SCRIPTURE

Create in me a clean heart—Psalm 51:1–13
Don't practice your piety in public—Matthew 6:1–6

Holy Week / Easter

See resources for Lent, Holy Week, and Easter in Chapter 14, pages 83–90.
See resources on Jesus in Chapter 15, pages 148–160.

See section on Lent, Holy Week, and Easter in Chapter 14, pages 83–90.

Pentecost

(Resources also appropriate for Week of Prayer for Christian Unity and World Communion Sunday.)
See resources on the church in Chapter 15, pages 112–128.

APPROPRIATE SCRIPTURE

The day of Pentecost—Acts 2:1–41

One Great Hour of Sharing

"A Litany for a Hungry World," page 103
"Christ Is Present in the Hungry Poor," page 151

APPROPRIATE SCRIPTURES

I was hungry and you fed me—Matthew 25:31–46
If you sow sparingly—2 Corinthians 9:6–11
Share with the hungry—Isaiah 58:6–11

Earth Day

See resources on creation and ecology in Chapter 15, page 137–148, especially the prayers and
"A Statement of Faith," page 142
"A Liturgy for the Earth," page 145
"How Can You Sell the Sky?," page 143

APPROPRIATE SCRIPTURE

The earth is the Lord's—Psalm 24
A new heaven and a new earth—Revelation 21:1–7

Christian Family Week / Festival of the Christian Home

"Litany for Peace With Justice," page 104
See resources on parents, friends, and school in Chapter 15, pages 169–177.
"A Litany of Faith and Courage," page 169
"You Have Called Us Forth," page 130
"God Is Our Father," page 193

APPROPRIATE SCRIPTURE

Honor your father and mother—Deuteronomy 5:16

Independence Day (July 4th)

(Resources also appropriate for other national holidays of a patriotic nature.)
If your theme is peace, see the section on peace and justice in Chapter 15, page
99–112.
A new hymn, "For living saints," in Chapter 15.

APPROPRIATE SCRIPTURE

The choice is life or death—Deuteronomy 30:11–20a
Breaking down walls—Ephesians 2:12–22
The law's fulfillment—Matthew 5:17–24

World Communion Sunday

(Resources also appropriate for Pentecost and the Week of Prayer for Christian
Unity.)
See resources on the church in Chapter 15, pages 112–128.
See resources on peace and justice in Chapter 15, pages 99–112.

APPROPRIATE SCRIPTURE

There is one body and one Spirit—Ephesians 4:1–6
When we dwell in unity—Psalm 133

Access Sunday

"Voices From Private Worlds," page 107

APPROPRIATE SCRIPTURE

He was despised and rejected—Isaiah 53:1–5, 10–11
All things united in Christ—Ephesians 1:3–11, 15–23
The man born blind—John 9

World Food Day

"Litany for a Hungry World," page 103

APPROPRIATE SCRIPTURE

Give food to the hungry—Isaiah 58:1–12
I was hungry and you fed me—Matthew 25:35–40
Feeding the 5,000—John 6:5–14

World Order Sunday

See resources on peace and justice in Chapter 15, pages 99–112.
"Invocation," "Doxology," and "Commissioning," pages 113–114
"Confession of Sin," page 114

Swords into plowshares—Micah 4:1–4
Love your enemies—Matthew 5:43–48
The new world in Christ—2 Corinthians 5:16–21

Stewardship Sunday

See resources on personal religious living, pages 128–137, and on creation and
ecology, pages 137–148, especially, "A Liturgy for the Earth," page 145.

APPROPRIATE SCRIPTURE

Let your light shine—Matthew 5:12–16
God or Caesar—Mark 12:13–17
The Christian life—Romans 12:1–11

Bible Sunday

APPROPRIATE SCRIPTURE

Jesus' family—those who hear the word—Luke 8:19–21
Be doers of the word—James 1:22

Thanksgiving Sunday / Thanksgiving Day

See resources on Thanksgiving in Chapter 14, pages 90–92.
"Enter With thanksgiving," page 189
"Fasting for Peace and Justice," page 109

APPROPRIATE SCRIPTURE

David gives thanks—1 Chronicles 16:1–13
A psalm of thanksgiving—Psalm 92
Jesus' gratitude—Matthew 15:32–39; 26:26–30

Youth Sunday

See resources on personhood in Chapter 15, pages 160–168.
See resources on parents, friends, and school in Chapter 15, pages 169–177.

APPROPRIATE SCRIPTURE

Whom shall I send—Isaiah 6:1–8
Remember your Creator in the days of your youth—Ecclesiastes 12:1–10
Let no one despise your youth—1 Timothy 4:11–16

Notes

Part One

1. Floyd Shafer, "Clowns in Worship? What Next?," *Modern Liturgy* 8, no. 5 (August 1981).
2. Margaret Palmer Fisk, *The Art of the Rhythmic Choir* (New York: Harper & Brothers, 1950), 3.
3. Albert Edward Bailey, *The Gospel in Art* (Philadelphia: Pilgrim Press, 1946).

Part Two

1. In *Sisters and Brothers Sing!,* ed. Sharon Emswiler and Tom Neufer Emswiler (Normal, Ill.: Wesley Foundation), 193. Used by permission.
2. James O. Gilliom, unpublished call to worship. Used by permission of the author.
3. Harry Emerson Fosdick, quoted in *Worship With Youth,* by J. Martin Bailey and Betty Jane Bailey (Philadelphia: Christian Education Press, 1962), 217–218. (Hereafter referred to as Bailey and Bailey.)
4. Howard Thurman, Howard Thurman Foundation.
5. Leslie F. Brandt, *Psalms/Now* (St. Louis: Concordia Publishing House, 1973), 191. Adapted from *Psalms/Now* by Leslie Brandt. Copyright © 1973 by Corcordia Publishing House. Used by permission.
6. In *God-With-Us: Resources for Prayer and Praise,* ed. Miriam Therese Winter (Nashville: Abingdon Press, 1979), 105. From *God With Us* by Miriam Therese Winter. Copyright © 1979 by Medical Mission Sisters, Philadelphia, PA. Used by permission of the publisher, Abingdon Press.
7. Allen Hackett, *Prayers of a Pastor* (Honolulu: Woman's League of the Central Union Church (UCC), 1951). Used by permission of the author.
8. In *Contemporary Worship Resources for Lent* (Lima, Ohio: C.C.S. Publishing Co., n.d.), 53. Copyright by C.C.S. Publishing Company, Lima, Ohio. Used with permission.
9. Herbert Yeager, prayer. Used by permission of the author.

10. Loretta Whalen Force, in *God-With-Us: Resources for Prayer and Praise*, ed. Miriam Therese Winter (Nashville: Abingdon Press, 1979), 55–56. "Paradox" by Loretta Whalen Force from *God With Us* by Miriam Therese Winter. Copyright © 1979 by Medical Mission Sisters, Philadelphia, PA. Used by permission of the publisher, Abingdon Press.

11. Oliver Huckel, from "I Prophesy Sunrise," in *Worship With Youth*, by Bailey and Bailey, 217–218.

12. From *A Book of Worship for Free Churches* (New York: Oxford University Press, 1948), 57. © 1948. The Board of Home Missions of the Congregational and Christian Churches, 1948.

13. Jane Merchant, in *Farm Journal*, Nov. 1, 1955, in *Worship With Youth* by Bailey and Bailey, 222. Used by permission.

14. Roger Lovette, in *Ventures in Worship*, ed. David J. Randolph (Nashville: Abingdon Press, 1970), vol. 89–90. "For Thanksgiving" by Roger Lovette from *Ventures in Worship*, vol. 2, by David J. Randolph. Copyright © 1970 by Abingdon Press. Used by permission.

15. Bill Barrett, O.F.M., in *Youth* magazine (New York: United Church Board for Homeland Ministries), January 1982, 49–51.

16. Francis of Assisi, arranged by Barbara Fuchs, in *Worship With Youth* by Bailey and Bailey, 193–194.

17. Roger L. Shinn, in *Keep in Touch: Prayers, Poems, Images, and Celebrations by and for the Young*, ed. Herman C. Ahrens, Jr. (New York: Pilgrim Press, 1978), 86–87.

18. Materials for Peace With Justice Week (New York: National Council of Churches, 1985). Used by permission.

19. *Ibid.* Used by permission.

20. Annemarth van Lelyfeld, in *Tune In*, ed. Herbert C. Ahrens, Jr. (New York: Pilgrim Press, 1968), 66–67.

21. Distributed by the Fellowship of Reconciliation. Used by permission.

22. Adapted from Mae Hurley Ashworth, in *Heads Bowed Together: Worship Resources on Reconciliation*, comp. Ann Simon (New York: Friendship Press, 1966), 55–58. Used by permission.

23. Adapted from Worship Resources, 8th Assembly (1985), Christian Conference of Asia, 10 New Industrial Road #05.00, Singapore 1953. Used by permission.

24. *Rural Life Prayers* (New York: National Council of Churches, Division of Church and Society). Used by permission.

25. Karl Bernard Ritter, in *When We Pray*, ed. Wilhelmina Rowland (New York: Friendship Press, 1961), 8. Adapted by permission.

26. Worship materials used at the 15th General Synod of the United Church of Christ, 1985.

27. *Ibid.*

28. *Ibid.*

29. *Ibid.*

30. Adapted with permission from the ecumenical service of worship used by the General Assemblies of the Presbyterian Church in the U.S. and the United Presbyterian Church in the U.S.A., May 24, 1981.

31. *Ibid.*

32. In *When We Pray,* ed. Wilhelmina Rowland (New York: Friendship Press, 1961), 55.

33. E.W. Mueller, "Litany from Order for Worship for Rural Life Sunday" (New York: National Council of Churches, Division of Church and Society, 1959). Adapted by permission.

34. *Peacemaking Through Worship,* Presbyterian Peacemaking Program, n.d. Used by permission.

35. *Ibid.*

36. *Ibid.*

37. A Summary Affirmation of the Presbyterian Church, used in an ecumenical service of worship at the General Assemblies (PCUS and UPCUSA) May 24, 1981, in Houston, Texas. United Presbyterian Church in the U.S.A., Office of the Stated Clerk. Used by permission.

38. Adapted from Donald G. Miller, *The Nature and Mission of the Church* (Richmond, Va.: John Knox Press, 1957). Used by permission.

39. William Charles Walzer, in *International Journal of Religious Education* (New York: National Council of Churches), September 1956. Adapted by permission.

40. Donald G. Miller, *The Nature and Mission of the Church.* Used by permission.

41. *Peacemaking Through Worship.*

42. Words by Herman F. Reissig, music "Sine Nomine" by R. Vaughan Williams. Used by permission.

43. Words by Jane Parker Huber, music "In Babilone" arranged by Richard R. Frey, 1981. To be published in *A Singing Faith* (Philadelphia: Westminster Press, 1987). Used by permission.

44. Margaret Chaplin Anderson, in *World Outlook* (475 Riverside Drive, New York, N.Y. 10114). Used by permission.

45. Adapted by Barbara Fuchs, in *Worship With Youth,* by Bailey and Bailey, 174–176.

46. Adapted from "Witness of a Postman," *Christian World Facts, 1958–59* (New York: Friendship Press). Friendship Press, New York, copyright 1985. Used by permission.

47. Norman W. Jackson, in CWS *Connections,* October 1985, p. 10. Used by permission.

48. Ruth Kaufman, in *A.D.* magazine, November 1976. Used by permission.

49. Randy E. Dyer (McNeil Island Federal Penitentiary, Steilacoom, Wash.), in *A.D.* magazine, November 1976. Used by permission.

50. Percy R. Hayward, from *International Journal of Religious Education,* in *Worship With Youth,* by Bailey and Bailey. 111. Used by permission.

51. Walter Rauschenbusch, in *Prayers of the Social Awakening* (New York: Pilgrim Press, 1910), 47. Used by permission.

52. Francis of Assisi, in *Worship With Youth,* by Bailey and Bailey, 108–109.

53. "The Joy of Creation," from *Jesus Christ: The Life of the World* (Geneva: World Council of Churches, 1983), 15. © 1983 World Council of Churches. Used by permission.

54. John Baillie, *A Diary of Private Prayer* (New York: Scribner, 1952), 125.

55. *Ibid.,* 91.

56. This statement of faith is a blend of readings from Pierre Teilhard de

Chardin—*The Phenomenon of Man* (New York: Harper, 1959); *The Divine Milieu* (New York: Harper, 1960); "The Center Letter," no. 1 and no. 5, in *Letters From a Traveller* (New York: Harper, 1960)—with portions of the Statement of faith of the United Church of Christ. "A Statement of Faith," first printed on pages 11–12 of the program book for the Ecumenical Event, Cleveland, Ohio, November 5–7, 1981, celebrating the 30th anniversary of the National Council of Churches.

57. Frieda Haddad, in CWS *Connections*, October 1984, p. 15. Used by permission.

58. Nella Braddy, preface of *Midstream*, by Helen Keller (Garden City, N.Y.: Doubleday & Co., 1929). Used by permission.

59. Adapted from an order of service prepared by a group of Native American women and distributed by Church Women United.

60. Robert V. Moss, Jr., prayer. Used by permission of Junia Moss Jones.

61. Edith Lovejoy Pierce, in *Christian Century*, March 16, 1955. Copyright 1955 Christian Century Foundation. Reprinted by permission from the March 16, 1955 issue of *The Christian Century*.

62. Adapted from Edward J. Brady, S.J., in CWS *Connections*, August 1984, p. 23. Used by permission.

63. Albert Edward Bailey, *The Gospel in Art* (Boston: Pilgrim Press, 1946). © 1944 by the author.

64. *Ibid.*

65. *Ibid.*

66. In *A Book of Worship for Free Churches*. © 1948 The Board of Home Missions of the Congregational and Christian Churches.

67. In *The Kingdom, the Power, and the Glory* (New York: Oxford University Press). Used by permission.

68. Boynton Merrill, in *A Book of Worship for Free Churches*, 355.

69. Stuart G. Oglesby, *Prayers for All Occasions* (Atlanta: John Knox Press). Used by permission.

70. Richard K. Avery and Donald S. Marsh, in *Avery and Marsh Songbook* (Port Jervis, N.Y.: Proclamations, 1973), 10. Used by permission of Hope Publishing.

71. Marilee Scroggs, in *Bread for the Journey*, ed. Ruth C. Duck (New York: Pilgrim Press, 1981), 72.

72. Herman C. Ahrens, Jr., ed. *Keep in Touch: Prayers, Poems, Images and Celebrations by and for the Young* (New York: Pilgrim Press, 1978).

73. Frederick Buechner, in *Wishful Thinking: A Theological ABC* (New York: Harper & Row, 1973), 51. © Frederick Buechner.

74. Herman C. Ahrens, Jr., in *Youth* magazine (New York: United Church Board for Homeland Ministries).

75. Brenda Reimer, in *Keep in Touch*, ed. Ahrens, 41.

76. Herman C. Ahrens, Jr., in *Tune In*, ed. Ahrens (New York: Pilgrim Press, 1968), 88.

77. J. Donald Hughes, in *The Hymn Society of America*, (Forth Worth, Tex.: Texas Christian University, 1983). © Copyright 1955. Renewal 1983 by the Hymn Society of America, Texas Christian University, Fort Worth, TX 76129. Used by permission.

78. Lois Horton Young. *A Litany for Growing Up* (Philadelphia: Christian Education Press).

79. William W. Finlaw, in *Youth* magazine.

80. Jim Taylor, in *An Everyday God* (Nashville: The Upper Room), 77ff. Reprinted by permission for *An Everyday God* by James Taylor, co-published in the U.S. by the Upper Room, Nashville, and in Canada by Wood Lake Books, Inc., Box 700, Winfield, B.C. VOH 2CO.

81. Herman C. Ahrens, Jr., in *Tune In*, ed. Ahrens, 72.

82. Leslie Anne Weishaar, in *Youth* magazine (New York: United Church Board for Homeland Ministries).

83. Nevin C. Harner, *I Believe: A Christian Faith for Youth* (New York: Pilgrim Press, 1950), 122–123. Adapted by permission.

84. In *Our Christian Beliefs* (Philadelphia: Christian Education Press, 1954), 55.

85. Nevin C. Harner, *I Believe*, 121.

86. Adapted from John H. Huston, in *Worship With Youth*, by Bailey and Bailey.

87. James Montgomery (1771–1854), in *Great Companions*, comp. R.F. Leavens, Vol. 1 (Boston: Beacon Press, 1927).

88. Ancient Daybreak Liturgy, Eastern Orthodox Church.

89. This material is drawn from the Lima Liturgy used at the 6th Assembly of the World Council of Churches in Vancouver, Canada, in 1983, and from the Worship of the 13th and 15th General Synods of the United Church of Christ in Rochester, New York, in 1981 and in Ames, Iowa, in 1985.

90. Jerry Paul, in *Worship: Inclusive Language Resources* (St. Louis: United Church of Christ, Office for Church Life and Leadership, 1977), 11. Copyright 1977. Used by permission.

91. Adapted from Clarice Bowman, *International Journal of Religious Education* (New York: National Council of Churches). Used by permission.

92. In *Sisters and Brothers Sing!*, ed. Emsweiler and Emsweiler, 169. Used by permission.

93. Family Week materials (New York: National Council of Churches, Department of Adult Work and Family Life). Used by permission.

94. From Liturgy of the Russian Orthodox Church, Version IV, in *Jesus Christ: The Life of the World* (Geneva: World Council of Churches, 1983), 117. Used by permission.

95. Linda Warwick, in *There Are Rainbows* (Honolulu: Hawaii Conference of the United Church of Christ, Task Force on Women, 1981), 13.

96. Art Solomon, Ojibway Nation, in *Jesus Christ: The Life of the World* (Geneva: World Council of Churches, 1983), 71.

97. Carol Bernard, in *Worship: Inclusive Language Resources* (St. Louis: United Church of Christ, Office for Church Life and Leadership, 1977), 37. Copyright 1977. Used by permission.

98. Ruth C. Duck, in *Bread for the Journey: Resources for Worship*, ed. Duck (New York: Pilgrim Press, 1981), 21.

99. *Ibid.*, 29.

100. Jerry Paul, in *Worship*, 19. Used by permission.

101. In *Worship With Youth*, by Bailey and Bailey, 102.

102. Author unknown, in *Jesus Christ: The Life of the World* (Geneva: World Council of Churches, 1983), 95.

103. Augustine, quoted in *Worship With Youth*, by Bailey and Bailey, 95.

104. Book of Common Prayer, quoted in *Worship With Youth*, by Bailey and Bailey, 95–96.

105. *Sarum Printer* (1558), quoted in *Worship With Youth*, by Bailey and Bailey, 103.

106. Robert G. Kemper, benediction. Used by permission of the author.

107. Michael Bausch, in *Worship: Inclusive Language Resources* (St. Louis: United Church of Christ, Office for Church Life and Leadership, 1977), 49. Copyright 1977. Used by permission.

108. Ruth C. Duck, in *Bread for the Journey*, ed. Duck, 70.

109. Adapted from Robert G. Kemper, benediction. Used by permission of the author.

110. The Boran of Kenya, "Let Me Pass the Day in Peace," in *No Longer Strangers* (Geneva: World Council of Churches, 1983), 32. © World Council of Churches Publications, Geneva, Switzerland, 1983. Used by permission.

111. Wheadon United Methodist Church Worship Commission, Evanston, Ill., in *Bread for the Journey*, ed. Duck, 39.